Murder Weapon

A thriller

Brian Clemens

Samuel French — London
www.samuelfrench-london.co.uk

Copyright © 2012 by Brian Clemens
All Rights Reserved

MURDER WEAPON is fully protected under the copyright laws of the British Commonwealth, including Canada, the United States of America, and all other countries of the Copyright Union. All rights, including professional and amateur stage productions, recitation, lecturing, public reading, motion picture, radio broadcasting, television and the rights of translation into foreign languages are strictly reserved.

ISBN 978-0-573-11262-1

www.samuelfrench.co.uk
www.samuelfrench.com

For Amateur Production Enquiries

United Kingdom and World excluding North America

plays@samuelfrench.co.uk
020 7255 4302/01

Each title is subject to availability from Samuel French, depending upon country of performance.

CAUTION: Professional and amateur producers are hereby warned that MURDER WEAPON is subject to a licensing fee. Publication of this play does not imply availability for performance. Both amateurs and professionals considering a production are strongly advised to apply to the appropriate agent before starting rehearsals, advertising, or booking a theatre. A licensing fee must be paid whether the title is presented for charity or gain and whether or not admission is charged.

The professional rights in this play are controlled by Samuel French Ltd, 24-32 Stephenson Way, London, NW1 2HD.

No one shall make any changes in this title for the purpose of production. No part of this book may be reproduced, stored in a retrieval system, or transmitted in any form, by any means, now known or yet to be invented, including mechanical, electronic, photocopying, recording, videotaping, or otherwise, without the prior written permission of the publisher. No one shall upload this title, or part of this title, to any social media websites.

The right of Brian Clemens to be identified as author of this work has been asserted in accordance with Section 77 of the Copyright, Designs and Patents Act 1988.

CHARACTERS

Jessica Bligh, Chief Constable, late 40s
Inspector Fremont, male, around 45 or 50
Constable Walters (male)
Charley Mirren, about 50, looks older
Hugo, around 35
Diane, about 30
Paul, well over 40

The roles of Constable Walters and Paul may be played by the same actor

SYNOPSIS OF SCENES

The action of the play takes place in the conservatory of Dysart Hall

ACT I
SCENE 1 About 11.30 p.m. on a Saturday
SCENE 2 10 p.m., the same Saturday
SCENE 3 Midnight, the same Saturday
SCENE 4 Some time later, Sunday morning

ACT II
SCENE 1 Sunday, about 3 p.m.
SCENE 2 Later that night

Time — the present

Other plays by Brian Clemens
published by Samuel French Ltd

Anybody for Murder? (with Dennis Spooner)
The Devil at Midnight
The Edge of Darkness
Holmes and the Ripper
Inside Job (or Murderous Liaisons)
Shock!
A Sting in the Tale (with Dennis Spooner)
Strictly Murder
Without Trace (or Murder Hunt)
Will You Still Love Me in the Morning? (with Dennis Spooner)

This play is dedicated to my dear friends,
Raymond and the lovely Wendy

ACT I

The conservatory of Dysart Hall. About 11.30 p.m. on a Saturday

This was once a proper conservatory in the Victorian manner, but transformed into an area more suitable for today's modern living — without losing the essential "garden" atmosphere. French doors lead out to a terrace and the grounds and gardens beyond: near to them are "hi-tech" shelves bearing some hi-fi equipment and a shelf containing some printed plays. There is a low, rug-covered sofa and, most important of all, a chair. This chair could be one of the hanging type, like a womb-like egg, or a high-backed swivel chair — either way, it must be able to turn on its own axis and be of such dimensions that, if one were seated in it, legs tucked up and facing away from the audience, it would appear to be empty. (NOTE: If staging permits, this could be the chair behind the desk)

Elsewhere is a small, good quality desk, with a suitable chair behind it. There is a door nearby. There is also a small, iron-work table; on the table is a telephone, a tray of drinks and glasses and a bagged pistol in a clear plastic bag. To one side of the area there was once an "eyesore" of old plumbing, heating pipes, etc., but these have now been virtually blotted from sight by a clever designer who has erected a kind of lattice screen way above head height. There is nothing anachronistic about the screen which is covered with artificial flowers, plants, and possibly the use of floral printed paper. Behind this screen there is enough space to hide. On the opposite side to the screen is a door that leads through to the rest of the large house that is Dysart Hall

The french doors are wide open, and standing near to them is Jessica Bligh. She is in her late 40s, but is still a handsome woman with a good figure. At this time she wears a fashionable trouser suit (or, if preferred, bearing in mind she has some vigorous action to carry out later, a dress). Her hair is longish and lustrous — there is no way anything masculine about her

Bligh moves to pull the doors closed, then turns and moves to the table and picks up the bagged pistol — clearly seen through the clear plastic bag as Bligh turns it over in her hands, examining it

Inspector Fremont enters through the house door. Fremont is around 45 or 50; he is hard, world-wise, and a touch weary too. He is a very good copper indeed, but he has seen it all, and doesn't much like any of it. He wears a shabby top coat over equally well-worn clothes — he could do with a haircut and probably a drink as well, and when he speaks it is clear that his education probably ended at the local comprehensive

Bligh Well, Inspector, what do you think?
Fremont I think it's gone past eleven-thirty, and time we were home, ma'am.
Bligh That's it? You have no other comment?
Fremont Like what?
Bligh We-ll. This is the first time I have actually attended a murder investigation, but —
Fremont Just plain murder, ma'am. There's nothing to investigate, is there? Body's on its way to the morgue (*he jerks his thumb towards the house door*) ... we've got our man. And ... (*he glances at his watch*) if I'm lucky I could be tucked up in bed by twelve.
Bligh I'm disappointed in you, Inspector. A policeman of your experience. We have a unique opportunity here.
Fremont Opportunity?
Bligh Yes. Here we are at the scene of the crime, a crime that took place less than an hour ago. A hot trail — piping hot. Shouldn't we take advantage of that? Investigate, interrogate, before it cools off? Isn't that how it's done? Isn't that "the form", Inspector?

Fremont sighs, then takes the bagged gun from Bligh

Fremont Under normal circumstances. But look, ma'am, .22 pistol. Three chambers fired, and three bullets in the victim. And once ballistics get hold of this —
Bligh (*interjecting*) I've no doubt that it is the murder weapon.
Fremont Then that's it, isn't it, ma'am? You saw who was holding it — damn near caught him in the act — then add to that his statement —
Bligh (*interjecting*) That wasn't a statement, it was a garbled outburst.
Fremont Nevertheless, he more or less confessed —
Bligh It was gobbledegook.
Fremont What else do you expect? The man's bloody barmy!
Bligh I think we should have him in again, Inspector.
Fremont For what? His prints are all over his gun — got to be ... and don't forget his previous record — he's done it before — and the same *modus operandi*, with a gun. And if that's not enough, there YOU are,

ma'am, practically an eyewitness. It's the most open and shut case I've ever had to deal with.
Bligh I still think we should question him again. Properly.
Fremont For God's sake, ma'am, it's getting on for midnight ...
Bligh Are you anticipating turning into a pumpkin, Inspector?

Fremont stares at her

Let's have him in again.
Fremont By the book is it, ma'am? The military way?
Bligh If you like, yes.
Fremont Very well. (*He consults his watch, and then moves to the house door*) Constable Walters!

Uniformed Constable Walters appears in the doorway

Walters Inspector?
Fremont Let's have the prisoner.
Walters Right, Inspector.

Walters exits

Bligh now moves to scuff a foot where the body once lay, then touches the swing chair, sets it turning around on its axis so that we see it clearly

Walters ushers in Charley — then exits

Charley is about 50, but looks much older, a man with an air of despair about him. He is a "loser" from way back, a man imbued with an anxiety, a fear and a blind respect for authority. His hands are cuffed in front of him, and when he speaks he has a faint, quite pleasant trace of Irish accent, but along the way has picked up some cockney vernacular. We shall find that, occasionally, when under stress, Charley puts a hand to his brow or temples as though to soothe a chronic headache

Bligh Charles ... Mirren?
Fremont Charley. Everyone calls him Charley.
Bligh Sit down, Charley. And let's have those cuffs off.

Fremont reacts to this

Fremont If you're doing this by the book —
Bligh The book — humanely interpreted. Now let's have them off or is he a black belt in karate?

Fremont unlocks the cuffs. Charley sits down, rubbing his wrists. Bligh produces a small voice recorder and switches it on

Bligh Now, Charley, I shall be recording this interview. I want you to tell me, in your own words, exactly what happened here tonight.
Charley If I can remember.
Bligh Do you know who I am?
Charley No.
Bligh I am the new Chief Constable of this county. Jessica Bligh.
Fremont Bligh. You know, like the captain of the *Bounty*?
Bligh Except I am ex-army not navy. I think you already know Inspector Fremont.
Fremont Course you bloody do. Was me who arrested you last time, wasn't it? Ten years ago. I was just Constable then.

Bligh reacts

(*Seeing Bligh's face*) Oh, sorry, ma'am.
Bligh Well, Charley, it looks as though you have committed murder here tonight.
Fremont Looks?! Oh, sorry, ma'am.
Bligh Right. Your name is —— ?
Charley (*looking at Fremont*) You know who I am.
Fremont She wants it all official — army fashion — *proper*. Tell her your name, Charley. Your full name.
Charley Charley. Charles Henry Mirren.
Bligh And your present address?
Charley I've got a room over the pub.
Fremont Which pub, Charley?
Charley Well, YOU know ...
Fremont The name and the street.
Charley Oh. *Rose and Crown*. Church Street.
Bligh Your occupation?
Fremont Well, that's easy. Burglar. Petty thief. That's when he's not killing people!

Bligh gives Fremont a hard look

Bligh What do you do for a living?
Charley Well, I ... I haven't got a job at the moment. But I'm looking. But before ... I did a bit of building work, and window cleaning.
Fremont Handy that, wasn't it, Charley? For casing the job? Peering in people's windows — sussing out what they had worth nicking?

Act I, Scene 1

Bligh Inspector Fremont, I would prefer that you remain silent during this interview, unless you have something relevant to add.
Fremont (*snapping to attention*) Yes, ma'am!
Bligh Charles Mirren — Charley — it is true, is it not, that you shot and killed a man here tonight?

Charley, under growing stress now, looks at her haplessly

  I'll repeat the question. Is it not a fact that tonight you —
Charley (*overriding*) No, it isn't going to work. I wasn't supposed to be caught here ... you'll make the connection now, you will. Put two and two together ... you'll find out about me and George —

Bligh and Fremont are astonished by the outburst

Fremont George? Who's George?
Charley I've got to tell the truth I have. The whole truth —
Bligh And what is the truth?
Charley I didn't kill him. I didn't kill no one.

Bligh and Fremont exchange a look

Fremont (*accusingly at Bligh*) Oh, that's bloody dandy that is. Few minutes ago — gobbledegook or not — we had a nice verbal "cough" — a confession to be built upon ... and now he's taking it all back!
Bligh Is that correct? Are you now saying you did NOT commit a murder here tonight?
Charley I couldn't kill anyone.
Bligh Dammit, man, I saw you with the gun in your hand!
Charley I didn't kill him.
Bligh Then why the devil did you say you did?
Charley It was for George. I was trying to protect George ... I wasn't supposed to be caught ...

Bligh, her consternation growing, looks at the cynical Fremont

Bligh (*to Charley*) You don't deny that you broke in here tonight?
Charley No. I mean yes. You see, I didn't break in exactly. The door was open.
Bligh Very well, you entered these premises furtively and uninvited with intent to commit a felony.
Charley No ... You see, I was going to —
Bligh (*overriding*) You came through that door, carrying a gun. This gun!

Charley No.
Bligh For pity's sake, man —
Charley (*overriding*) I didn't bring the gun. That was already here. In that drawer.

Fremont, who has so far been abdicating from the proceedings, becomes alert and looks at Bligh

Fremont Did you know they kept a gun?
Bligh No. (*To Charley*) So, you started to ransack the place and you came across the gun.
Charley No, I didn't come across it. I knew it was there. I didn't ransack nothing —
Fremont Knew the gun was there, did you, Charley? That's what you came for, was it? A handy tool to go along with the crowbar and picklocks?
Charley No.
Fremont You came here to steal the gun and whatever else you could lay your hands on. Then suddenly you were disturbed, the door opened and a man stood there — and there YOU are, Charley, with a gun in your hand, and no compunction about using it. I mean you're an old hand with guns, aren't you, Charley ...? So you shot him.
Charley No —
Fremont (*overriding*) You shot him three times. He caught you stealing and you killed him.
Charley No, it wasn't like that. I didn't come here thieving, that wasn't in my mind at all!

Bligh and Fremont exchange a puzzled look

Bligh Then why did you come here, Charley? If it wasn't to steal, then why?

Charley looks from one to the other helplessly

Are you saying that you came here with intent to murder!?
Charley In a way. Yes.
Fremont Now, that's more like it — and about wraps it up, ma'am.
Bligh Nonsense!
Fremont But you heard him —
Bligh (*overriding*) If the shooting wasn't done in a blind panic, if he came here with deliberate intent, then why? What possible motive could he have had?

Fremont Perhaps somebody paid him to do it. Is that why you killed him, Charley?
Charley I didn't kill him. I couldn't kill anyone.
Fremont Come on, Charley, this is Inspector Fremont you're talking to. You *couldn't*?!
Charley I ... I thought about doing it. I'll admit that. Even went so far as to say I'd do it. But I didn't.
Fremont You were here. You were seen.
Charley It's all a mistake. If you'll just listen — let me have my say.
Bligh I want you to have your say, Charley. I want you to tell me everything that happened, everything you can remember — in chronological order.

Charley regards her blankly. Fremont sighs and consults his watch

Fremont She means from the beginning. So let's have it, Charley. And make it quick.
Charley It was ... six weeks ago they let me out.
Fremont (*consulting his notebook*) Six weeks and two days.
Charley Was it? It's all mixed up in my mind ... A letter! Yes, that's it, they gave me a letter to ... someone.
Fremont Addressed to Doctor Blake. From the prison authorities, it was part of the parole stipulation that Charley "undertook to receive psychiatric treatment". Though what this doctor stuff has to do with what happened here tonight I don't know.
Bligh Well, if we give him a chance, he'll tell us. Won't you, Charley?
Charley I ... I dunno, it's all mixed up ... I forget things.
Bligh No need to rush it ... take it easy. Let's start with the exact date you visited Doctor Blake?
Charley I don't remember ... Pride Street! Yes, that means something ... but I don't know what.
Fremont Twenty-eight Pride Street is where Doctor Blake is situated.
Charley There was a big brass plate outside! Wasn't there? Told you it's all mixed up.
Fremont Twenty-third of June you were due there. Your appointment was for twelve-thirty.
Charley I got there early! Yes, it's coming back to me now ... no it isn't. It's no good.
Bligh Perhaps if we can pretend? It may help jog your memory ... I imagine Doctor Blake had a desk, didn't he?
Charley Yes.
Bligh (*moving to the desk in the room*) Like this one?
Charley A bit ... no, not really ...

Bligh A desk is a desk, Charley ... just try to imagine it ... on that day ... Concentrate ...

As she talks she moves to the light switches and turns off the main lights so that only the desk and the immediate area is lit. Her voice becomes soft and caressing

   Think back, Charley ... you came to the door, knocked and ...
Charley I didn't have to knock. The door was already open ... I just pushed it wider and went in ...
Bligh And what? A receptionist sitting there?
Charley No, there was nobody ... but there were papers scattered about like someone had left in a hurry ...
Bligh So then what happened ...? Take it step by step, Charley.

During this Fremont has reacted with exasperation — turning to astonishment when Bligh's method seems to work

Charley There was another door facing me, that was open too, so I went in ...

Charley now enters the light of "the office" — starting to live out his story

Bligh Was that when you met Doctor Blake for the first time?
Charley No. That office was empty too — but then he came in through the side door.

The door (to the rest of the house) opens and Hugo enters, his face hidden by the open book he is studying, which is in fact a desk diary. Hugo is around 35. Stocky, well built, darkly handsome, with (hopefully) a full head of hair — wearing a dark suit, and, from time to time, thick-rimmed spectacles, he looks almost a stereotype of a psychiatrist

He didn't see me at first.

Note: this to be conceived so that Charley is first standing then sitting in a chair at the end of the desk, rather than across from it, else he will have his back to us all the time!

Hugo lifts his head from the book, reacting to Charley

Hugo Who the devil are you?

Act I, Scene 1   9

Charley Doctor Blake?
Hugo Well, what do you think? Says "Doctor Blake" on the door, doesn't it? (*He pats the desk*) Doctor Blake's desk. His chair. And me sitting in it. Don't I look like a psychiatrist? Ah, just a moment ... (*With a flourish, he puts on the spectacles*) That better? Now who are you?
Charley Charley Mirren, sir.

He produces an official envelope and extends it to Hugo, who merely regards it

  I'm not supposed to be here until twelve-thirty, but I'm early. I'm sorry. Very sorry.
Hugo Mirren?
Charley Yessir.

Hugo puts the diary down and starts to run a finger down it

Hugo "C" for Charley?
Charley Yessir.
Hugo Aha. "C. Mirren." Says it right here. Twelve-thirty. "C. Mirren". So I suppose I shall just have to see Mirren, eh? You'd better tell me what it's all about.
Charley It's all in there, sir. (*He again extends the envelope*) I just got out of prison, sir.
Hugo Did you now? That IS interesting. (*He finally takes the envelope, opens it, and scans the contents*) Been a bad boy, have we? And what have you been up to, eh? A bit of flashing? Petty theft? Poking horses' eyes out? Good God!

He reacts to the official papers, looking from them to Charley and back again, with a new appraisal

  Fascinating. Utterly fascinating.

Now his manner starts to undergo a subtle change. Gone is the banter, to be replaced with an attitude more fitted to a brilliant psychiatrist

  You'd better sit down, Charley. You don't mind if I call you Charley? No couch I'm afraid. Couches are apparently out this year. Anyway, they smack of cliché don't you think?

Charley, a bit bewildered, sits in the chair obliquely facing the desk

I've dealt with the common criminal before of course. Yes. But you, Charley, you are a most uncommon criminal.
Charley (*vaguely reassured*) They said you'd be able to help me, sir.
Hugo I shall certainly try. I'd offer you some tea, but my receptionist ... well, you know how staff are these days? No, perhaps you don't. Locked away, what was it ...? (*He consults his papers*) Ten years. A long time, Charley.
Charley It seemed longer.
Hugo I'll just bet it did. Said with subjectivity, Charley. Straight from the horse's mouth, eh? The real McCoy! This is a new experience for me, one to be savoured! Here I am, sitting across the desk from — *able to stretch out and touch* — a real live murderer. A cold-blooded multi-killer. You'll forgive me if I say that you don't much look the part, Charley. No, you look very ... ineffectual ... hard to believe that you have committed murder.
Charley As a matter of fact, sir ——
Hugo (*overriding*) Now don't tell me you were innocent, Charley. I'd hate to have you disappoint me.
Charley Disappoint ...?
Hugo We are going to be very close, Charley. I feel it. So don't you go letting me down ... Now then, what was it like to kill another human being, Charley? How did it feel? Elation? Drained of all aggression — a catharsis? Oh, this is such fun! Or did it just leave you feeling cold and empty? A real live murderer!
Charley But, sir, I didn't ——
Hugo Oh, but you did. Not only did you do it, but you made a full confession afterwards. It says here, clearly in black and white; you confessed to murdering your wife and two children. A boy of six, the girl barely eighteen months ...
Charley No, sir ...
Hugo With a shotgun! You *blasted* them away! What a terrible thing to do, Charley! But you must tell me all about it at first hand. Every tiny detail.
Charley Please, please. (*He buries his head in his hands*) They said you'd help me.

Hugo regards him

Hugo (*more gently*) All right, Charley. Charley? Pull yourself together now.
Charley I'm sorry, sir. Very sorry.
Hugo We have to do these things you know. We psychiatrists. Shock can be a therapy too. Stop snivelling now.

Act I, Scene 1   11

Charley Yes, sir. Sorry, sir.
Hugo Don't worry, I won't attack you like that again. No more shocks, eh? We'll just talk. Quietly. And you can tell me all you know. Share your experience with me.
Charley I'll try, sir.
Hugo I know you will. (*Very gently*) Now — why did you do it?
Charley I ... I don't know, sir.
Hugo Oh, come now, *you know*. Somewhere in your subconscious ...
Charley I'm sorry, very sorry.
Hugo For pity's sake stop saying you're sorry all the time! (*More gently*) I want to be your friend, Charley. And I want you to trust me. Do you understand?
Charley I think so, sir.
Hugo Now let's get some background. Some essential detail ... to help me understand your motivations, eh? And once I've understood them, I can interpret them — and thereby lies a cure. It says here that you might have been paroled last January. But you weren't. Why not?
Charley (*muttering*) I stole some stuff ...
Hugo What was that, Charley? Speak up, please.
Charley I stole some stuff from the prison shop.
Hugo What did you steal? Money? Cigarettes?
Charley Chocolate.
Hugo Eh?
Charley Chocolate bars.

Hugo is becoming more and more the stereotyped psychiatrist, twiddling his glasses, peering closely at Charley, sitting back, linking his fingers, etc.

   But I made a full confession. To the trusty, AND to Father Syson.
Hugo Very strong on confessions, aren't you, Charley?
Charley But I never mentioned George!
Hugo George?
Charley Not even to Father Syson. I know it's a sin not to tell the whole truth, but I never told them about George.
Hugo Who ... is George?
Charley My cell mate.
Hugo I see. And why would you have mentioned George in connection to the chocolate bars?
Charley Because they were for him. I stole them for him.
Hugo He made you steal them?
Charley No, no, of course not. George was my friend,
Hugo You shared a cell together and he was your friend. What kind of friend?

Charley He *listened* to me. Not like the others, *he* didn't think I was crazy. He listened and ... and we talked. And played cards, and when his wife brought him something, he'd always share with me. Always.
Hugo How does this link up with the chocolate bars?
Charley George and me had a row. Over nothing important — over which book was his and which was mine. He said he was going to put in for a transfer.

Hugo regards him blankly

A *transfer*. Request to move out of my cell ... *our* cell — and go somewhere else. I couldn't let him do that! George was my friend, I *depended on him*. D'you see?
Hugo Charley, I may be a bit dense ... but the chocolate bars?
Charley They were for George. Potty for chocolate he was. So I thought ... if I got him some chocolate ...
Hugo You could bribe him to stay.
Charley I'd patch up the quarrel. And I did too. Never a cross word after that.
Hugo Nevertheless something compelled you to confess to the crime ...
Charley I dunno why, but I had to. Funny — I've got so many big things locked away inside of me, but I had to go and confess to that small one.

Hugo regards him happily

Hugo You're a real character, Charley, do you know that? Now then, tell me about "George" — this man you became so dependent upon. What kind of man is he?
Charley He's a bit younger than me, but much brighter — educated is George.
Hugo Aha, the subjugation of the lesser intellect by a superior one.
Charley Sir?
Hugo Your George, the clever fella with a sweet tooth — and your best friend in prison, eh?
Charley Yessir.
Hugo Understandable. Proximity of two people denied the comforts and excitements of the outside world. Is he still in the nick?

Charley looks shifty; he touches his brow

Hugo Well, is he?
Charley No, sir. He was ... released three months ago.

Hugo Touched a nerve have I, Charley?
Charley He said he'd write. Said he'd meet me when it was my turn. He didn't do either ... and ... and when I went to the address he'd given me ... he'd gone. No idea where. P'raps — p'raps he had an accident.
Hugo So, your chocky bar friend let you down. Lots of people let you down, don't they, Charley?

Charley nods

Got many friends on the outside, have you?
Charley No, sir. Not a one. After what I did you see ...
Hugo Ah, yes, wife and two kids. Your popularity plunged alarmingly I should imagine. You miss George, don't you?
Charley Yes, sir.
Hugo What do you miss most about him?
Charley Him setting me right, sir.
Hugo Oh?
Charley Yessir. You see, if I had a problem, something bothering me, then I'd get one of my headaches ... can't think proper when they come, sir ... everything gets ... all mixed up. George always puts me right though, told me what to do.
Hugo Trusted him implicitly, did you?
Charley Yessir.
Hugo Well ... he's obviously abandoned you, so now you'll have to confide in me. You'll have to trust me. Think you could do that?
Charley Oh, yessir. I will. I mean I do. You can help me, can't you, sir?
Hugo D'you know, I rather think I can. Come on, now, tell me all about your murders ...
Charley I'd rather not, sir ...
Hugo And I would rather that you did. (*Consulting his watch*) But not here. Have you had lunch, Charley?
Charley No, sir.
Hugo (*standing up*) Neither have I. Now then, why don't we continue this over a beer and a sandwich?
Charley Whatever you say, sir.

Hugo regards him for a moment

Hugo Yes, whatever I say. But this "sir" business isn't conducive to a friendlier relationship, and that's what I want. And it suddenly occurs to me that, oddly enough, my middle name is "George" too. So why don't you call me that, eh? George. OK?

Charley Yes ... George.
Hugo Excellent. Come on then.

Hugo starts to move away, then hesitates, returns to pick up his appointment diary from the desk, then moves to exit through door

(*Off stage*) Come on, Charley!

Charley remains, is about to move when Bligh turns lights back on again, and the spell is broken

Bligh Then what?
Charley After that I met him every week, sometimes two or three times a week. I liked that, liked talking to him, he was such a good listener ... it was like ... like going to confession, except that he didn't give me no Hail Marys or read the wrath of God at me ... he understood.
Bligh So you've been regularly meeting Doctor Blake over the past six weeks?
Charley Yes.
Bligh At his consulting rooms.
Charley We never went there again. He said it was too ... formal. Said I'd been instituted — institushunned —
Bligh Institutionalized?
Charley Yes, that's it. Said I'd had enough of that in prison.
Bligh So where did you meet?
Charley Pubs. Cafés. The park — and a couple of times at his home.
Bligh His home?
Charley Why here of course. In this very room!

Bligh and Fremont exchange a look. Fremont touches his head to indicate a screw loose

Fremont Paroled into psychiatric care, ma'am.
Bligh Charley, when was the last time you met Doctor Blake here?
Charley Thursday just gone.
Bligh Day before yesterday. And in this very room?
Charley Wasn't supposed to be here. He'd arranged to meet me at the pub — *The Bricklayers* — but he didn't turn up. I started to get worried. It wasn't like him to let me down. *He never let me down.* And he was always on time, on the dot. So I ... I came here to look for him. That's when it happened — *started* to happen. Tonight — the gun — everything.
Bligh When you met Doctor Blake here?
Charley Yes.

Bligh I want you to be very careful about this, Charley. I want your exact recollection of that meeting.
Charley We-ll. I came up the drive, heading for the front door I was, then I saw him standing in the garden. So I went over to him.
Bligh The garden, Inspector.

Fremont sighs, and now grabs Charley's arm and takes him to the french doors

Whereabouts in the garden was Doctor Blake standing?
Charley Over there — just by that tree.

Bligh nods

Bligh Inspector.

Bligh exits — Fremont and Charley follow to exit and disappear from sight

Bligh (*off stage*) He greeted you and brought you in through the french doors?
Charley (*off stage*) Yes.
Bligh (*off stage*) What time was it?
Charley (*off stage*) Just after two. A fine sunny day.

Now the lighting changes from night to day — until the room and the garden beyond is illuminated by a fine sunny day. We hear some birdsong

Hugo enters through the french doors. He wears tweedy, casual clothes. Charley enters behind him

Charley I was worried sick. Thought you might have had an accident. It was awful, George. I suddenly felt like I used to feel — before I met you. Alone. Helpless.
Hugo I'm sorry, Charley.
Charley Anyway, it's all all right now. Here you are ... here I am.
Hugo Yes.
Charley (*proudly*) I'm sleeping well at last, George. Not a single nightmare in the past few days. Nor any headaches.
Hugo That's good.
Charley What's wrong, George?
Hugo Wrong?
Charley There's something wrong, I can tell.

Hugo No, no, everything's fine, just fine.

As he talks, he takes a cigarette from a box on the shelves — puts it in his mouth, then begins to pat his pocket for matches

Charley *George!*

Hugo stares at him

You don't smoke. Not any more. You told me, you gave up months ago.

Hugo removes the cigarette from his mouth, and then stares at it

There *is* something bothering you, and you should talk about it. That's what you keep telling me.
Hugo Not your problem, Charley. Or, for that matter, any of your business.
Charley Maybe not, but, after what you've done for me these past few weeks ...? If I can help, I'd like to.
Hugo These past few weeks? We've come a long way, haven't we? Since that first meeting? But it was just doctor and patient then. Now ...?
Charley Mates. (*Then, a bit abashed*) Well, that's how I like to think of it.
Hugo And it's how I like to think of it, too, Charley. Friends. Confidants ...? (*Then, he suddenly shakes his head*) No. Why should I burden you? God knows you have enough of your own problems ...
Charley How many times have you told me, "a problem shared can be a problem solved"? You never know. I MIGHT be able to help ...
Hugo (*hesitating*) Thanks, Charley, but what could you do? What can anyone do!

And, with a terrible, inner anguish, he moves to stand, clenched fists on the table, head bowed

Charley (*at a loss, but desperate to help*) George!? Please, George.
Hugo "Physician heal thyself". It's ironic, Charley, these past weeks I've helped pull you up out of the mire, helped put your life in order ... whereas, when it comes to me ...!
Charley George, you've got to tell me!

Hugo regards him — then moves away — paces, comes to a decision, and finally

Act I, Scene 1   17

Hugo It's Diane.
Charley Your wife? But you've told me about her — how much you love her and your life together —
Hugo (*interjecting*) I worship her. She *is* my life.
Charley Well, then —
Hugo She's having an affair. Oh, Charley, I'm losing her!

Charley regards him — at a complete loss for a moment

Charley Come on. How do you know ...?
Hugo I know. *I've seen them!* (*He has an internal struggle, then gets a grip on himself*) Remember when we met last week?
Charley At the café? Yes.
Hugo When you turned up you told me you had an interview for a job and you had to leave early ...
Charley (*defensively*) Well, I couldn't let you know before — the offer only came through as I was —
Hugo (*interjecting*) You left early, *and I returned here early*. That's when I saw them, Charley. Right here. I stood at the doors and watched them — watched *him* — kissing her — pawing her ...
Charley Who?
Hugo His name is Paul. Paul Tulliver. A social friend. I trusted him. *I trusted her.*
Charley What did you do?
Hugo Nothing. Absolutely nothing. I ... I just couldn't stand to watch them. *Me*, who spends his life urging others to face up to reality! I just ... slunk away, like a beaten dog. I felt sick.
Charley That's understandable. The shock and all ...
Hugo I made a friend of him, Charley, welcomed him into my home, and he repays me by seducing my wife!
Charley The bastard! I'd like to bump into him one dark night!
Hugo I thought of that. But knowing Diane, she'd probably rush to bathe his wounds.
Charley How long's it been going on, d'you know?
Hugo Some time I imagine. They meet in town, or here, on those days when they know I'm busy with you, or another patient. Then they sneak back here and ... Oh, Charley, what am I going to do!?
Charley I ... I dunno. But I tell you one thing, you've got one good friend who won't let you down!
Hugo I know, Charley.
Charley I hate to see you like this, George.
Hugo At my wit's end? Unable to cope?
Charley No, no, not you. You'll think of something. Won't you?

Hugo I *have* been thinking.
Charley There, y'see?
Hugo I have a cousin in America. Did I ever tell you that? No. He's in the same profession and making a fortune. He's often asked me to go out there and set up with him.

It takes some moments for this to penetrate Charley's mind. Then:

Charley America? But you wouldn't do that, would you?
Hugo It would be an answer, wouldn't it? New country, new life. Put all this behind me.

Hugo moves to stand by the french doors for a moment — staring off

Charley But not forever. I mean America's thousands of miles away, how would I get to see you?
Hugo I'm afraid you wouldn't, Charley.

Hugo moves back to Charley

Charley But that's no answer, that's ... that's running away, that's what that is. I thought you said you loved your wife.
Hugo I do.
Charley Well, that'd be giving her up, wouldn't it? Without even *trying*.
Hugo (*getting a sudden thought*) When they know I'm away!
Charley Eh?
Hugo They come here when they know I'm away, seeing you ...
Charley What are you talking about?
Hugo Today, Charley. I'm not supposed to be here today, am I? I'm supposed to be meeting you.

Charley stares at him for a moment — then makes the connection

Charley Here! You don't think they might ...
Hugo I don't know, but there's a chance, isn't there?

At this moment we hear Diane's laughter off stage, from beyond the french doors. Hugo hurries over to peer out, then reacts, spins round

Oh my God, it *is* them! Coming this way!
Charley Then that's it, you've got to have it out with them now.
Hugo No, no, I couldn't ... not yet ... not now ...

Act I, Scene 1

Charley But, George ——
Hugo (*overriding*) Quick, get out of sight. Here ... and keep quiet.

Hugo grabs Charley and tugs him away so that they both exit behind the screen, to remain there, in hiding

A moment later Diane enters, followed by Paul

Diane is a very attractive woman of about 30. She wears a sweater and slacks that heighten her sexiness. Paul is a bit of a surprise. He is well over 40 and, although pleasant enough, he presents a comfortably middle-aged image that is not at all the passionate lover we might have expected. (He may also have facial hair ... if being doubled). Diane, clutching some sheets of writing paper in her hand, laughing, runs into the area, pursued by Paul. He catches her by the sofa, and they fall upon it, to playfully wrestle and embrace, and then they suddenly succumb into a long and passionate kiss, from which they eventually emerge, both a bit breathless

Paul Are you sure your husband won't be coming back? I feel a damned fool saying that —— !
Diane (*interjecting*) Darling. *Please.*

She kisses him, silences him

> He's seeing that weird Charley man I told you about. He won't be home until this evening, which means we have the whole, beautiful afternoon ahead of us.

Paul grabs the papers, studies them quite closely

Paul (*curiously stilted*) Darling, I have to tell him about us.
Diane No! I'll tell him. But in my own time, in my own way. Otherwise, I don't know what he might do.
Paul I can take care of myself.
Diane He keeps a gun you know.
Paul Eh?
Diane Over there, in that drawer.

Paul finally tosses the papers back to Diane

Paul And you think he might use it against me, eh?

Diane No, he'd never do that. But he might just put that gun against his own head ——
Paul (*interjecting*) He's a psychiatrist for God's sake, he must spend half his time counselling against suicide.
Diane Darling, I know him better than you, and there are things you *don't* know. He's volatile, impulsive, he *could* do it.
Paul Take his own life ...?
Diane He's tried it before!

Paul reacts, regards her. She nods grimly

> Four years ago he became desperately depressed. He took some pills. Of course it was all hushed up; if it had got into the papers his practice would have been finished. So you see, darling, why I must tell him at the right moment, in the right way. I couldn't have that on my conscience.

Paul Why did he try it? Was it because of you? Another lover?
Diane Darling, I'm not promiscuous, I don't go hopping in and out of bed.
Paul You have with me.
Diane Because I *love* you ... Now let's forget it for a while, what he doesn't know can't harm him. Will you come over Saturday night? He's going to be away the whole weekend.
Paul But don't you have to go out too?
Diane The local choral society. As a patron I have to put in an appearance, but I should be back by ten. (*She moves to the french doors*) I'll leave these unlocked for you, you can slip in, have a drink, and then, when I get back ...
Paul I'll be waiting.

Diane's tone undergoes a subtle change, as though she has finished with that part of the conversation. She tosses the papers down

Diane Thanks, darling.

Paul leans back against the sofa — seeming to completely relax now

Paul Right, what now?
Diane Let's go to bed.
Paul In the middle of the afternoon!?
Diane I'd like to. I want to. Don't you?

Diane lightly kisses him

Paul Terribly decadent.
Diane But nice. I promise you, it will be very, very nice.

He embraces her, and then, his arm around her shoulders, they exit through the house door

The stage is empty for a long moment, then finally Hugo and Charley enter from behind the screen. Hugo is utterly stunned by what he has seen and heard, and Charley acutely embarrassed at having been a witness to it. He is at a loss for some moments

Charley She's got to be barmy. He's years older than you, and no oil painting either. He couldn't hold a candle to you, George.
Hugo You saw, you heard them. He's got my wife, and woven a spell around her. (*He moves to stare up at the ceiling*). And now ... Right now!
Charley You've got to go up there, George! Have it out with them. It's the only way.
Hugo No.
Charley But, George ——
Hugo (*overriding*) Once I do that, it's irrevocable. They'll know I know and be forced into a decision. She'll leave me, and what will I do then, Charley? Beg? Plead? You look upon me as some kind of god — a surrogate father who can solve everything. Well I can't, and I'm no god, I'm human.
Charley Well, you've got to do *something*.
Hugo Yes. (*He paces away to stand facing upstage and at the drawer that contains the gun. Then, affecting a lightness of manner*) I'm sorry about today, Charley, mucking up our meeting. Very sorry. Still, we can have our usual session next week, can't we, old chum? Yes. (*He turns to face Charley*) You'd better run along now.
Charley When next week?
Hugo Oh, er ... let's say Monday, shall we?
Charley You always go to the hospital on Mondays.
Hugo All right, then, Tuesday. Yes.
Charley What time?
Hugo Usual time. In the pub, eh?
Charley You sure you're going to be all right?
Hugo Yes. Don't worry. I'll work something out.
Charley You never told me you once tried to top yourself.
Hugo It's something I try never to think of, or talk about.
Charley It's a mortal sin it is. Suicide.
Hugo Charley, you don't have to worry.

Charley Don't I?
Hugo No, you don't. I just need some time alone, that's all — think things through. You run along now, there's a good chap. I'll see you next week.
Charley Tuesday.
Hugo Yes, yes, Tuesday. Now please go!
Charley I might phone you tomorrow, see how you are.
Hugo That's it. You do that. Goodbye, Charley.

Charley hesitates, then exits through the french doors

A moment, and then Hugo lets his real anguish show again. He stares up at the ceiling, his hands clenching and unclenching, then finally he turns, moves to the drawer and takes out the pistol. He regards it for a long moment, again looking up at the ceiling, and then he makes up his mind. He puts the muzzle of the gun into his mouth

Charley enters at a run, from where he has been hiding just beyond the french doors

Charley No!

He grabs Hugo's gun hand, pulls it down, and then, after a brief struggle, disarms him

I thought so. I bloody thought so! That's no answer.
Hugo Isn't it?
Charley I told you, it's a mortal sin. About the worst thing you could ever do.
Hugo It's none of your damned business!
Charley Oh, isn't it? If you topped yourself where would I be, eh? Where would that leave me? Alone, that's what, I'd be alone again. How'd I cope without you, George? (*He gestures with gun*) This is potty, and *I'm* supposed to be the potty one!
Hugo Perhaps you're right.
Charley Course I am.
Hugo Paul. That's who I should kill. Yes. Saturday night. You heard them, coming here again, isn't he? For another assignation, another quick leg-over. *With my wife! Yes.* He thinks I'm going to be away, but I won't, I'll be standing here, waiting in the dark, and when he comes through those doors I'll pump bullets into his foul face!
Charley No, George.
Hugo Give me the gun.
Charley No.

Act I, Scene 1

Hugo *Give me the gun.*

His tone is so imperious that, for a moment, Charley hesitates, the inferior under the orders of his superior again. But he JUST manages not to obey Hugo, just manages to hold on to the gun

Charley I can't, George. I'm sorry ... don't make me.
Hugo *Charley* ——
Charley (*desperately — overriding*) They'd know straight off it was you who did it. You'd be inside in a twinkling, your feet wouldn't touch.
Hugo I don't care what happens to me, don't you understand that?
Charley Oh, you'd care soon enough. I had ten years of it, don't forget. Believe me, you'd care.
Hugo But it didn't stop you, did it, Charley? You must have felt as I do now; blind, impotent rage. *You* pulled the trigger on them, didn't you?
Charley These past weeks I've tried to tell you about that, tried to explain ...
Hugo All right, Charley, you win. You've persuaded me. You can go now. And take the gun with you if it makes you feel any better.

Charley is "thrown" by this complete change of attitude — and he is immediately suspicious of it

Charley No. I'm not leaving.
Hugo But I've told you ...
Charley Soon as my back's turned you'll try again, I know you will. With pills or a razor or something. I'm not leaving.

Hugo regards him then, to Charley's consternation, he finally, completely breaks, close to tears

Hugo What can I do? What else can I do!?

Charley, as usual when faced with a crisis, is at a loss. His limited brain is working overtime

Charley I can do something.
Hugo Eh?
Charley I can do something for you for a change. Yes. Why not?

As the idea starts to take shape in his mind, he hefts the gun

I'll get rid of him for you.

Hugo stares at him

This Paul Tulliver. Won't be you waiting for him here Saturday night. It'll be me. With this. (*He hefts the gun*) Yes. You won't be involved at all. You're going away for the weekend, right? And that's just what you'll do, go away, far away — and stay away ... and I'll take care of things for you here.

Pleased with himself, Charley almost swaggers now

Yes. Who's going to make the connection? ... And anyway, I've got no reason to kill him, have I? Except to help you, and that'll be our secret. Let me get rid of him for you, George.
Hugo I can't let you.
Charley (*overriding*) After all. I'm an old hand at it, aren't I? It's like you keep on saying, I've done it before.

Out of sheer desperation, Charley is summoning a strength of purpose we have not seen before

I've got to do it. It's the only way, George.
Hugo No ——
Charley (*overriding*) *Yes*. I'm gonna do it for you — for us. And we'll both get away with it! Then everything will be just like it was, won't it, George? We can have our little sessions again, can't we? I'll talk, you'll listen and ... and ... and help me. The two of us. Mates. You've got to trust me, George — I won't let you down.
Hugo If I agreed to this I'd be as guilty as you, an accessory.
Charley But who'll know, except us?
Hugo (*softly*) It would be a bond between us that nothing, no one could ever break.
Charley That's right, George. We'd be like ... like them red Indians when they cut theirselves ...
Hugo Blood brothers.
Charley *Yes*.
Hugo No, even if I thought it would work, I couldn't let you ——
Charley (*interjecting*) It will work. Got to.

Hugo regards him, then Charley hefts the gun

Saturday night. Ten o'clock and it'll all be over. This Paul won't bother you any more, I promise you.

Act I, Scene 2

Hugo paces away, the idea taking hold

> We would have to think it through, Charley. Make sure nothing had been overlooked. The gun! You'd have to give it to me — you'd have to leave the gun here.

Hugo makes as though to take the gun, but Charley evades him

> You're on parole, liable to be picked up and searched at any time. If they found you carrying that gun it would all be over ...

Charley regards Hugo for a moment, then finally allows him to take the gun back. Hugo regards it, then turns and moves to replace it in the drawer and firmly closes the drawer again

> This way would be safer. Keep the gun here where it belongs, then you would arrive before Paul Tulliver. Pick up the gun and ... That's the way it should be done. If we were to decide to go through with it.

Hugo and Charley regard each other

Slow fade to black-out — and, a beat or two after the black-out

CURTAIN

SCENE 2

Almost immediately, the CURTAIN *rises again on the same*

The set is still virtually in black-out, save for some moonlight filtering through the french doors. The swivel chair is turned away from us. The set is empty

A torch shines against the french doors, then Charley opens them and enters. He carries the torch and is in a state of tension. He flashes the torch around the room, then moves to open the drawer and take out the gun. Charley moves as though to start positioning himself facing the french doors, then reacts to a small sound and, out of the swivel chair, a man's legs descend to the floor. Although turned away from us, clearly someone is seated in it

This scares Charley as much as it does us; he spins round, gun ready, pointing his torch towards the chair

Charley Tulliver? Paul Tulliver. (*He advances warily towards the chair*). You don't know me. I'm George's friend. Doctor Blake's. Got a gun I have. And I'm bloody well going to use it! On you. You understand? You've got to leave her alone, see? George's wife — you've got to go now and never come back. You've got to leave them alone ... or else ... *Look at me when I'm talking to you*!

He grabs the chair, tugs it and sets it turning slowly on its axis to face us. At this moment the off stage clock begins to chime 10 — and we see that, seated in the chair, eyes open and staring, bloody from three bullet wounds, is Paul. He is dead!

Charley is frozen into immobility. The chair stops its revolve and then Paul, very slowly, folds forward to fall out of the chair and lie face down on the floor. Charley is still unable to move, and during this period, the clock finishes chiming 10. Finally Charley moves and, gun in hand, he moves to stand over Paul and direct his torch down on him

We hear a door slam off stage, and almost immediately:

Diane (*off*) I insist you have one drink, it's the very least I can do after making you sit through all that.

Charley is still so shocked that the voice does not immediately get through to him. Then it does and he snaps off his torch

   Almost simultaneously, the house door opens and Diane enters and snaps on the main lights

Diane is smiling and wearing a formal evening dress. The smile wipes from her face as she sees Charley caught, standing gun in hand over the body of Paul. A moment later she screams

   Instantly Bligh dashes into the room behind her. She wears formal dress — over it, a coat or wrap

She takes in the scene as Charley, recovering from his initial shock, instinctively lifts the gun higher. Bligh plunges in to disarm him and sends him flying to the floor. Diane remains by the door — Bligh holds the gun, commanding the scene and looming over the fallen Charley, with the dead Paul nearby

CURTAIN

Scene 3

The same

As quickly as possible, the Curtain *rises again*

Again the set is in virtual black-out and illuminated only by moonlight through the french doors

The swivel chair is turned away from us. The set is empty. A torch shines against the french doors, then Charley opens them and enters. He carries a torch and is in a state of tension. He flashes the torch around the room, then moves to open the drawer and take out the gun

Charley moves as though to start positioning himself facing the french doors, then reacts to a small sound and, out of the swivel chair, a man's legs descend to the floor. Although turned away from us, clearly someone is seated in it. Charley spins round, gun ready, pointing his torch towards the chair

Charley Tulliver? Paul Tulliver. (*He advances warily towards the chair*). You don't know me, I'm George's friend. Doctor Blake's. Got a gun I have. And I'm bloody well going to use it! On you. I mean it! Unless you do as I tell you. You understand? You've got to leave her alone, see? George's wife — you've got to go now and never come back. You've got to leave them alone ... or else ... *Look at me when I'm talking to you*!

He grabs the chair, tugs it, sets it turning slowly on its axis to face us, and we see that Bligh is seated in it, without her coat/wrap

And at this moment the main lights are snapped on to reveal Fremont standing by the door and light switch. Bligh stands up from the chair. Off stage, the clock starts to chime 12

Bligh And that's exactly how you remember it?
Charley I swear to you, that's how it happened.

Bligh and Fremont exchange a look

   Well, you know the truth. You were there.
Bligh I came in after the event. Paul was already dead.
Charley I didn't kill him. On my mother's life ...

Fremont (*shaking his head*) Oh, Charley, Charley. You were caught bang to rights. Dead man on the floor, gun in your hand.
Charley I just came to warn him off. I couldn't kill anyone.
Fremont Yeah? Then who's that buried out at St Theresa's? Your wife and kids ... and now another one tonight.
Charley I only wanted to scare him.
Fremont Oh, you did that all right. Three bullets in the chest. You scared him right to death!
Charley No, he was already dead. (*He turns to Bligh*) He was already dead. Sitting there. (*Having a sudden thought*) And the clock was chiming. Ten o'clock! You must have heard it? And he was shot before ... well, you can tell that, can't you? These days you coppers can tell exactly when a —
Fremont (*interjecting*) Not to the nearest bloody second we can't. Anyway, in this case we don't have to. He was still warm, Charley, and you standing there holding a gun with three bullets fired ... (*To Bligh*) Why are we going on with this garbage? It's as plain as the nose on your face that he did it —
Bligh (*interjecting*) We're going on because I say so, Inspector. Because I want to.
Fremont But you near as dammit *saw* him do it for God's sake!
Bligh I didn't see him pull the trigger.
Fremont Well, that's a fine bloody point I must say ...
Bligh A point nevertheless.
Fremont Look, it's now way after midnight and —
Bligh (*interjecting*) And miraculously you haven't turned into a pumpkin, have you?

Fremont glares at her, but Bligh's voice is surprisingly placatory

Why don't you pour yourself a drink? I think it would be awfully good for you.

Fremont looks at the tray of drinks on the table, then hesitates

Fremont Could be construed as theft. Petty larceny.
Bligh Suppose I make it a direct order?
Fremont That'd help. (*He picks up a bottle, then hesitates*) Could be destroying vital evidence from the scene of the crime?
Bligh I'll take full responsibility, and a little soda with my scotch.

Fremont reacts and starts to pour two drinks. He hands a glass to Bligh, who regards him, then turns back to Charley

Act I, Scene 3   29

>   Well, Charley, you've admitted that you told this ... Doctor Blake that you were going to kill Paul.
> **Charley** No. I said I'd take care of things for him. It was never in my mind to shoot him ... just warn him off —
> **Fremont** What is your game, Charley? What do you reckon to gain from all this?
> **Charley** All what?
> **Fremont** (*to Bligh*) I mean he doesn't have to go for a diminished responsibility or an insanity plea ... halfway there already. The authorities already recognize he's nutty... so what's he after? (*Then, at Charley*) All what, Charley? All this damned nonsense, that's what. All these Doctor Blakes and star-crossed lovers! Why don't you come clean and give us a straight honest cough, Charley? Confess, tell the truth and then we could all go to bed!
> **Charley** I've told you the truth.
> **Fremont** (*in disgust*) I told you he was crazy — a screw loose. And that's not just me. The considered opinion of a panel of doctors. Why do you think they paroled him into psychiatric care?
> **Bligh** I didn't see him pull the trigger. *Nor did I hear any shots.*

Fremont stares at her, then strides over to the house door, to open and close it as he demonstrates

> **Fremont** Look at this door, must be an inch thick. And the walls? What would you say? Eighteenth century? None of your cavity brick then ... solid ... (*He shakes pistol in its plastic bag*) A .22 pistol. For target practice and ladies' handbags! Sound of a shot from that? Putt, putt, putt! No louder than a handclap. Why would you have heard any shots?
> **Bligh** I didn't hear any shots. But I heard the clock chime.
> **Charley** (*eagerly*) So did I!
> **Fremont** The clock's in the hall, near the front door, and just where you were entering the house.
> **Bligh** Nevertheless ... (*she turns to Charley*) There are still some points I want to go through with you again.

Fremont perceptibly groans. Bligh moves to the screen

>   You hid behind the screen and saw this man Paul embracing Doctor Blake's wife?
> **Charley** They were doing more than that. It was ... Well, I was embarrassed. With Doctor Blake — George — right there beside me ... it was a sad and terrible thing.
> **Bligh** The woman — his wife — her name was Diane?

Charley Yes.
Bligh The same woman who came into this room with me tonight?
Charley Yes.
Bligh Had you ever seen her before?
Charley I told you — last Thursday when she came in here with that Paul ...
Bligh I mean before that?
Charley Not in the flesh, but George had showed me photographs! He was always talking about her, always phoning her he was. Very much in love they were. It ... reminded me of my own wife.
Fremont The one you took a shotgun to!?
Bligh Where is Doctor Blake now? How can we get hold of him?
Charley I dunno. He was going away for the weekend. I told you, it was part of the plan, but I'm beginning to think ... (*He clams up*)
Bligh Yes, Charley? You are beginning to think what?
Charley Nothing.
Bligh You are beginning to think that perhaps he did not go away. That he returned here, murdered Paul ——
Fremont (*interjecting*) And stuck you with it. Left you to take the blame! Christ, I must be going potty too! *I'm* starting to believe it.
Bligh Well, Charley?
Charley I've told you everything that happened.
Bligh Oh, yes, you've told us that. Told us a detailed and quite extraordinary story, but there is still a great deal to be explained.
Charley Eh?
Bligh What does Doctor Blake look like?
Charley Oh, he's a very kind man. Very generous.
Bligh But what does he look like?
Charley Dark haired. Well-built — stocky, you know. Friendly face.
Bligh What age?
Charley About thirty-five.
Bligh Clean shaven?
Charley Yes.
Bligh And he wears spectacles?
Charley No.
Bligh But you said ——
Charley (*interjecting*) Well, yes. He *did* wear them. (*He frowns*) But just that one time — the day I met him in his office. I've never seen him wear them since.
Bligh Any distinguishing features ... anything unusual about him?
Fremont Oh, that'll be a lucky break, if he turns out to be a one-legged hunchback!
Bligh Inspector!

Fremont I'm sorry, ma'am, but I've been on duty since this afternoon. (*He glances at his watch*) Correction. *Yesterday* afternoon. And it's now well after midnight, and no, I am not going to turn into a pumpkin or six white mice or a golden coach, but I am tired. Bloody tired — and we keep on going over this fairy tale ...
Bligh Do you want to continue this tomorrow?
Fremont Frankly I don't see what there is to continue.
Bligh You don't find this story of Mirren's fascinating?
Fremont I think he's barmy. And if you care to cast your mind back, I thought he was barmy before I brought him in here!
Bligh What about the mysterious Doctor Blake?
Fremont I don't think he's particularly mysterious. I'm sure there was — *is* — a Doctor Blake, and that Charley was sent to see him. But the rest of it ...? The ravings of a lunatic, and I don't understand why we're still here talking about it!

Bligh hesitates, and Fremont seizes his opportunity to bear in

This Paul and Diane stuff? You know as well as I do that it's all a pack of lies, so why give any credence to the rest of it?
Charley I'm not lying. Paul and Diane, I saw them.
Fremont Oh, there was a Paul all right, and a Diane, that's about the only thing you got right, Charley.
Charley I don't understand. (*Looking at Bligh*) What's he mean?
Fremont Well, go on, ma'am, lay it on him. I've got second wind, I think I can stay awake long enough to see how he tries to wriggle out of this one!
Bligh Certain facts don't quite tie up, Charley.
Fremont You can say that again!
Charley But I've told you all I know.
Bligh Well, for one, this house does *not* belong to Doctor Blake.
Charley What? That can't be. I've met him here.
Fremont *You* say!
Bligh It does in fact belong to the Tullivers. Diane and Paul Tulliver.

Charley stares at her

Fremont Yes, Charley. The man you killed here tonight was not Diane Tulliver's lover — he was her husband!

Charley is utterly stunned. He looks to Bligh for confirmation

Bligh (*nodding*) They had been happily married for more than six years.

Charley But ... I don't understand ...
Bligh Nor do I, Charley, nor do I.
Fremont Never mind, perhaps the next head shrinker you see will make something of it. And I can promise you, Charley, there're going to be quite a few of those over the next twenty years or so.
Charley No, you're trying to trick me!
Fremont Why would we want to do that, Charley? We've got all we need on you. More than enough.
Charley What I told you is the truth — gospel!
Bligh And we have told you the truth, Charley.

Charley looks from Bligh to Fremont — he is stunned, confused

Charley Oh, sweet mother of Jesus! (*His hand creeps to his brow again*) I didn't imagine it all, did I? George and ... everything ...? I didn't get it wrong again, did I? Not again?
Fremont (*without malice*) I reckon you did, Charley.
Charley These headaches I've been having ... and nightmares — terrible nightmares.
Fremont That sounds more likely.
Charley No! It was real. He was real ... Oh, God. Oh, God, oh, God, oh, God ...

Bligh and Fremont regard him

Bligh Better take him away, Inspector.
Fremont Yes, *ma'am*! Come on, Charley ...

He helps Charley to his feet and puts the handcuffs back on

> *Fremont tugs Charley and leads him away — they both exit through the french doors*

Bligh stares after them, and then moves around the area, touching this and that salient feature, as though mentally checking up on Charley's story

Bligh Walters! Constable Walters!

> *Bligh exits through the french doors, pulling them half closed behind her*
>
> *A few moments later Diane enters through the house door. She wears a robe over a nightdress and looks distraught. She moves to pour herself a drink and sips it, her hand touching the phone, not sure whether*

Act I, Scene 3   33

to make a call or not. Then she glances around and sees that the french doors are not quite closed. She moves over to them and, at this moment, Bligh enters through the french doors

Diane Jessica! You scared the life out of me!
Bligh I'm sorry, Diane, I thought you were in bed. Didn't the doctor give you some tranquillizers?
Diane He did, but they're not working. But that's no wonder, is it? I needed a drink. You?
Bligh No thanks.
Bligh You really should be in bed.
Diane I did sleep for a while, then I turned over, put out my hand to touch him and — and ...
Bligh He wasn't there. I remember when Richard died, it was the proximity of him that I missed the most.
Diane I hoped it was a dream and that I'd wake up and ... I keep thinking about tomorrow and tomorrow and tomorrow ...
Bligh Diane. (*She moves to embrace Diane*) With each tomorrow the pain will lessen. Believe me ... I've been there.
Diane Why?
Bligh We may never really know, the man's deranged.
Diane Why did he come here? To rob us?
Bligh It looks that way.
Diane If only Paul hadn't been here, if he'd come with us ——
Bligh Wild horses wouldn't have dragged him. I remember him saying that once.
Diane Yes, he hated those choral evenings.
Bligh There is another way of looking at it. If you hadn't badgered me to come along, you might have returned home alone. He might have killed you too.
Diane I wish he had!
Bligh That's foolish talk.
Diane Oh, my darling Paul ...

She breaks again and Bligh consoles her

Bligh He wouldn't have approved of this.
Diane He loved life.
Bligh And lived it to the full. That's the only way to think of him. The man who loved and encouraged so much. It was he who pushed me into accepting this job, you know. "You'll be terrific at it, Jessica" he said. "And if you're not, well, they'll kick you out, but slap a damehood on you first — just to show there's no hard feelings!"

You too. Remember when the village players wanted you as Lady Macbeth and you didn't think you could do it, and Paul knew you could, and he was right?
Diane Lady M.
Bligh Eh?
Diane Lady M. Or "the Scottish play". You must never mention the actual name. It's supposed to bring ... bad luck.

Diane dissolves into tears again

God, I'm going to miss him. You must help me to be brave.
Bligh Let me call your sister.
Diane No. I have to get used to being alone now.
Bligh But not right away, and certainly not tonight. I could send a car, have her here within the hour ...
Diane I know you're only thinking of me, but I'd rather not see anyone just now. I'll be all right, I promise you.
Bligh You're sure ...?
Diane Yes.
Bligh Do you feel like talking? There are some questions that have to be asked. Routine, you understand ... but it might be better to get them out of the way. If you feel up to it?
Diane I'll try.
Bligh Well ... first, I didn't know that Paul kept a gun.
Diane You should, he had a firearms certificate, it's registered with your people ... or perhaps he registered it from our flat in town. Anyway, Jessica, of course you knew — you saw him use it!
Bligh What!?
Diane Last year, when I did that Durbridge play, and persuaded Paul to do a walk-on as a policeman. He used it then. With blanks of course.
Bligh Yes, I do remember. And he kept the gun here ...? (*She indicates the drawer*)
Diane Yes ... (*then*) was that the gun he used?
Bligh Yes. Had you ever seen him before tonight?
Diane The man who ...? No!
Bligh Do you think it possible that Paul knew him?
Diane How could Paul possibly know someone like that?
Bligh Was Paul here with you last Thursday?
Diane Of course. We were together every day.
Bligh I mean in the afternoon, around two o'clock?
Diane Yes, as a matter of fact. He took the afternoon off.
Bligh What did you do, do you remember?
Diane We talked for a while ...

Act I, Scene 3   35

Bligh What about?
Diane Oh, I don't know, this and that. And then we went to bed.

Bligh reacts, regarding her

> Yes, in the middle of the afternoon. Paul made a joke about it, "terribly decadent." We went to bed and we made love. I didn't know then that it would be the last time that we ... (*She falters*)

Bligh regards her sympathetically

Bligh That pre-empts my final question. Whether things were all right between you and Paul.
Diane Jessica, *I loved him*!
Bligh Of course you did.
Diane I'm sorry, I ... I don't think I can talk about him anymore just now.

Suddenly the phone rings. Diane turns to stare at it. It rings and rings until:

Bligh Hadn't you better answer that?

Diane just stares, mutely shaking her head. Bligh moves to pick up the phone

> It might be for me. Hello? Hello! They hung up. (*She replaces the phone, turns to Diane*) Now I think you must go to bed.

Diane I will in a moment, the pills and the drink are fighting, but I think one of them's starting to win. I need oblivion tonight.
Bligh If you don't find it, I will be here for a while yet.
Diane You're staying? For how long?
Bligh I'm waiting for a report from Constable Walters.
Diane I'll say good-night then.
Bligh Try to get some sleep.

Diane moves away

> Doctor Blake.

Diane stops, turns to stare at her

> Does that name mean anything?

Diane No. Should it?
Bligh Good-night, Diane.

Diane exits

Curtain

Scene 4

The same. Some time later

Bligh and Walters enter through the french doors. Bligh holds a sheet of paper

Bligh You're sure that these times are correct?
Walters Ambulance records, ma'am, and Blake's receptionist confirmed it ... though she didn't take too kindly to being woken up so late.
Bligh Which reminds me ... You should have been off duty hours ago.
Walters Don't worry, ma'am. (*He hesitates*) It's my first murder, ma'am.
Bligh Mine too ... You say nothing was touched — everything was exactly as Doctor Blake left it?
Walters Not according to his receptionist, there was a legal hiccup y'see. Mrs Blake's lawyer slapped some kind of restraining order on the place. They locked the office up.
Bligh Mrs Blake?
Walters The doctor's wife. A bit of a dragon by all accounts. She and the doctor had been living apart for some time, with a divorce in the offing. (*He hesitates*) There's another thing, ma'am ... it might not be important but —
Bligh (*interjecting*) Let me be the judge.
Walters I did a spot check, and I couldn't find a desk diary ... you know, any list of appointments ... I thought that was odd ... I can't see a busy psychiatrist functioning without one.
Bligh Neither can I. Well done, Constable.
Walters Thank you, ma'am.
Bligh When was Blake's office locked up, do you know exactly?
Walters Soon as they realized there was some problem over probate ... ten-thirty, Tuesday twenty-fourth of June.
Bligh The day after Doctor Blake died.

Curtain

ACT II

Scene 1

The same. Sunday. It is about three o'clock on a fine afternoon

On the table are some typewritten papers, with, acting as a paperweight, the bagged pistol

The stage is empty for a moment, then Bligh enters through the french doors. She now wears another outfit. She carries an old bucket full of sand and a small trowel. She puts the bucket down then stirs and scoops up some of the sand, letting it fall back into the bucket, and then taps it down fairly hard with the trowel. She consults her watch and, with an air of mounting excitement, moves back to the french doors and gazes off for a moment, then produces a white cotton glove and pulls it on to her hand. She reacts now as she hears the sound of a car approaching, again gazes out of the french doors, then pulls them firmly closed and hurries away to pick up the bagged pistol and remove it from the plastic. She then waits until ...

The doorbell rings

Bligh aims the gun into the bucket of sand and fires one shot then replaces the pistol in its plastic bag, then moves to stand just to one side of the french doors ... and waits

A moment or two later Fremont urgently rushes up outside the doors, starts to try and fumble to open them and Bligh steps into view to open them to allow Fremont to enter. Fremont is rather brightly dressed in obviously new golfing clothes

Fremont What the devil ...!?

Bligh regards him

   I heard a shot!

Bligh produces and gestures with the bagged pistol

Bligh Me.

Bligh pulls the doors wider

Come in, Inspector.

Fremont moves further into the area, still taken aback by proceedings

I fired as you rang the bell. And you heard it, didn't you? Heard it from outside, through these eighteenth-century stone walls?
Fremont Oh Christ. We're not back to all that again?
Bligh Thank you for coming.
Fremont Your message said urgent — backed by the voice of command and all that.
Bligh Looks as though I interrupted your golf.
Fremont How *do* you do it, ma'am? Must be a combination of observation and interpretation. I'm lost in admiration.
Bligh Have you been drinking, Inspector?
Fremont Just a couple of scotches to limber up my back swing. I am off-duty.
Bligh I know, and again, I'm sorry about your golf.
Fremont Oh, I don't care too much. I was three down anyway.
Bligh That doesn't sound so bad.
Fremont On the first hole!? I was glad to get away. Golf? I hate the game.
Bligh Then why on earth do you play?
Fremont I want to make Superintendent. It's either golf or the Masons ... We could have discussed it, you know.
Bligh Eh?
Fremont The dramatic gunshot. You didn't have to set me up like ... like some guinea pig!
Bligh You don't much like me, do you?
Fremont Not supposed to *like* you, am I, ma'am? Just blind obedience and toss in the odd genuflect? I can't believe this is how you conducted your military career. Brigadier and leader of men — lining up all the chaps on parade and asking, "Men, do you like me?" Anyway, it's mutual, isn't it?
Bligh No, oddly enough, it isn't. I know your record, and that's how I judge a man, by what he does, not by what he is. An excellent record and, as a matter of fact, I have some admiration for you.
Fremont But admiring's not liking, is it, ma'am? I expect I could have admired Ghengis Khan, but I don't think I would have liked him.
Bligh It's my army background, isn't it? You use my previous career like a club. Yes, that's it, you plodded your way up through the ranks, whereas I was appointed. Dropped on you from above, like a god.

Act II, Scene 1   39

Fremont Or a sack of potatoes.
Bligh My appointment may look to you like a sinecure, but I was qualified; I had long experience in military security. I can promise you, I am no fool.
Fremont It never for a moment crossed my mind that you were. (*He moves to pick up and examine the bagged pistol*) Yes, I heard the shot. But I was standing by the front door at the time. But you, ma'am ... last night ... were you still in the car? Was the radio playing? Did you blip the engine before you switched off? Was Mrs Tulliver laughing loudly? Which way was the wind blowing ...? Lots of things can mask a sound. No two situations are ever exactly the same. I mean for instance, you've just blasted off a gunshot, but Mrs Tulliver doesn't seem to have heard it — she hasn't come rushing in, has she?
Bligh As a matter of fact Mrs Tulliver isn't here. Her sister was here earlier and I insisted that Diane go home with her for a while.
Fremont Oh! Well, anyway, your little charade doesn't prove anything ...
Bligh I didn't regard it as conclusive, merely indicative. We'll get nowhere snapping at each other like this.

She regards Fremont a moment

> Inspector, I don't pretend to be subtle in my methods. I burned through the midnight oil last night, and was still working away early this morning — and *this* is what it's all about!

With an air of triumph, she hands Fremont a piece of paper. Fremont scans it, reacts, then looks at Bligh

> Well?

Fremont So Blake's dead, which means we can't question him. But that's not the end of the world, anything he might have said would only have been corroborative.
Bligh You're missing the point. Note the date and the time, Inspector, particularly the time!

Fremont again scans the paper, then

Fremont Yes, that is strange.
Bligh Strange? It's germane.
Fremont Doesn't change a thing as far as I'm concerned. In fact, it's just another confirmation — that Charley Mirren *is* round the twist. (*He grins*) I'd like to see what he has to say about *this*.

Bligh You will. In just a few minutes.

Fremont reacts

I've sent for him. He'll be here any moment.
Fremont Well, that's a mistake.
Bligh Mistake?
Fremont To have him here? I've always found that a cold, bare, prison cell, with your biggest, ugliest copper standing by the door, arms akimbo, is the most conducive way to —
Bligh (*interjecting*) I want it here.
Fremont Why?
Bligh I ... don't know. Put it down to intuition if you like. Woman's intuition. I feel the answers are here.
Fremont I see.
Bligh No, you don't see, do you?
Fremont No, ma'am. But that could be because I've attended a few hundred trials in my time, and I never once heard them call an expert witness on "intuition"!
Bligh There's more to it than that. (*She picks up the remainder of the papers from the table*) I had Mirren's statement transcribed — been through it half a dozen times, and there are anomalies ...
Fremont To put it mildly.
Bligh No, I don't mean inconsistencies in Charley's story, but *within* that story. If he were only half telling the truth —
Fremont (*interjecting*) That's where we differ, isn't it? *If* he's telling the truth — half, three-quarters or five-sixteenths! You give him the benefit of a doubt, whereas I *know* he's barmy — raving. He wouldn't know the truth if it jumped up and bit him.
Bligh Inspector —
Fremont (*overriding*) No, hear me out. I was arresting officer on Charley's first murder. Murders. Wife and two kids. Young kids. Have you got any children, ma'am?
Bligh I have a son, yes.
Fremont Could you imagine putting a twelve-bore to his head? That close it's like bursting a watermelon. Not pretty. And there was Charley, alternatively crying, praying, and shaking his head and saying, "It wasn't me." "*It wasn't* me!?" Holding the gun and covered in blood!? That's when I knew he was bonkers, and they have patted his bum and let him out after ten years, but I know he's still bonkers. And bloody dangerous. So perhaps this time they'll put him away, throw away the key, and we can all rest easy. Or do you have other plans?
Bligh I simply want the truth.
Fremont For Christ's sake, ma'am, what more do you need?

Act II, Scene 1   41

Bligh I want to be sure.

At this moment Walters and Charley enter, handcuffed together, to appear at the french doors

Bligh moves to admit them

Thank you, Constable. Remove the cuffs, and go and wait in the car.
Walters Yes, ma'am.

Walter removes the cuffs, then exits

Charley rubs his wrists, regards them, then announces

Charley I've decided to confess. Confess to everything.

Fremont and Bligh exchange a look

Fremont Everything?
Charley Yes. I killed him. That Paul. It was as you said, I broke in here, he surprised me and ... That's all you need, isn't it? Send me back now, won't they?
Fremont You're showing good sense at last, Charley. (*To Bligh*) I'll fetch Walters, we'll get it all down while he's in the mood.
Bligh No, not yet.
Fremont What do you mean, not yet?
Bligh I want to question him first.
Fremont He's coughed, prepared to make a full confession, and *you want to question him first.*
Bligh Last night you were protesting your innocence ...
Fremont And today he's changed his mind.
Bligh No.
Fremont Whose bloody side are you on!?
Bligh I am on the side of truth — justice.
Fremont Christ, I don't believe this!
Bligh And I'm not sure I believe him. What prompted this sudden change of attitude, Charley?
Charley I want to confess, get it over with.
Fremont That's the boy.
Bligh (*overriding*) Why? Have you decided to try and protect Doctor Blake again? To protect that other George in your life, is that your motive?
Charley N-no ... I just want to ——

Bligh (*overriding*) It's not necessary, you know. Doctor Blake — George — is beyond our reach now. He's dead.

Charley is stunned by this news for a moment. He looks from Bligh to Fremont for confirmation

Charley No.
Fremont That's right, Charley. He's gone to the big consulting couch in the sky!
Charley Doctor Blake ... George ...?

Bligh grimly nods

Oh my God. Oh, sweet Jesus and the holy Mary. (*He crosses himself*) I shouldn't have left him here that time. Oh, why'd he do it? I wouldn't have let him down. It *was* him then. He did kill that Paul ... and then ... How did he do it? Was it the pills or the razor?
Bligh Doctor Blake died of a heart attack.
Charley Praise God for that. He didn't take his own life then? Praise God ... but it was a visitation, that's what, a punishment ... it was meant. Yes, after he killed that Paul ...
Bligh He didn't kill Paul Tulliver. He couldn't have.
Charley But he must have. I mean, if he didn't, then who did?
Fremont Coupla seconds ago you were saying it was you! (*Then, to Bligh*) We had it all sewn up. Cut and dried.

Bligh picks up the papers

Bligh Charley, this is the transcript of the statement you made yesterday. I'd like to go back over a few things. Now, you first went to see Doctor Blake in his office on ... Monday, twenty-third of June?
Charley What's that got to do with —— ?
Bligh (*interjecting*) Yes or no, Charley?
Charley Well, yes ...
Bligh Your appointment was for twelve-thirty, but you arrived about ten minutes early, at twelve-twenty. Correct?
Charley Yes.
Bligh You are absolutely sure about that?
Charley Yes.
Bligh Monday, the twenty-third of June at about twelve-twenty. Now that *does* give us a problem.
Charley How?
Bligh Well, you see, Doctor Blake was in his office, seated at his desk

Act II, Scene 1   43

    when he suddenly collapsed. His receptionist phoned for an ambulance, and then rushed with him to the hospital, but he was found to be dead on arrival.

Charley Oh, George ... poor, poor George ...

Bligh The point is this. He collapsed at eleven forty-five that morning. The receptionist is very precise about that, and the ambulance men confirm the time she called. So, you see, Charley, on that morning when you say you first met Doctor Blake, either you got the time wrong or he had already been dead for nearly an hour!

Charley B-but, that's not possible!

Bligh Exactly my reaction. Impossible. But the facts are documented, and indisputable.

Charley I don't understand ...

Fremont Nor do we, Charley, and probably never will. It's another thing for the headshrinkers, but d'you know what I think? I think you did go to his office like you said, and went in and found it empty, so you sat down and then dreamed it all up ...!

Charley No, it wasn't like that —

Fremont (*overriding*) You couldn't take the disappointment of him not being there. It was another rejection ... because, you see, it made you feel important, didn't it, Charley, having your own head doctor? But suddenly you didn't. The office was bare. No doctor. So you made one up.

Charley It isn't true —

Fremont (*overriding*) You even wove in a bit of your old cell-mate — George — to give you security. So that's what you called this mythical doctor of yours — George. They call that compensating. Then, a few weeks later, when you broke in here, murdered Paul Tulliver and were caught at it, you resurrected your mythical doctor again, didn't you? As your bit of security blanket? You popped in George — Doctor Blake — as the reason for the murder you did, but you couldn't look at it in the cold light of reality! "It wasn't me." "It wasn't me." Just like that other time, Charley.

Bligh That's very good, Inspector. Psychologically sound too.

Fremont Why, thank you, ma'am!

Charley But it isn't what happened.

Fremont How do you know, Charley? With your mind all muddled up as it is, how do you know, or remember, what really happened?

Charley There was a Doctor Blake, he wasn't dead. I saw him ... Perhaps I got the day wrong! Yes, perhaps it was the day before ...?

Fremont Charley. The day before, you were still in the nick!

Charley I didn't imagine it. (*To Bligh*) I couldn't have done. Could I?

Bligh I'm baffled, Charley. To invent such an elaborate tale and then get the time wrong by less than an hour ...!? You'd have to be crazy to —

She stops short as she meets Fremont's eye. Fremont is nodding his head

Fremont That's right, ma'am.
Charley He was flesh and blood, as real as you are.
Bligh Not Doctor Blake.
Charley Yes!
Bligh No! Even your description doesn't match up. (*She consults the papers*) "Dark haired, well built, about thirty-five"? The real Doctor Blake was thin, bald, and nearly fifty!

Charley stares at her

Charley Then I am mad, aren't I? They should never have let me out.
Fremont Amen to that. You satisfied now, ma'am?

Bligh prowls restlessly around the area, making a vague gesture that could mean yes or no

We'll take him back then?

Bligh stops, to face Charley

Bligh It could not have been more inept. That's what I can't come to terms with. If it was all a lie — and I am not denying anything you've said, Inspector ... but, *if it was all a lie*, then why did he get it so wrong? In almost every detail; a doctor he could not possibly have ever met, a lover who turns out to be the husband. And even stupid things ...! He says Diane had an assignation here last night, whereas I know that she had invited me to a choral evening, and I would be bringing her home ...!
Fremont You know he isn't normal ...
Bligh But even madness has its own logic, doesn't it? Why so many mistakes? So blatantly obvious? Yet so meticulously detailed?
Fremont We'll probably never know, ma'am.
Bligh No, I doubt we ever will. I should have listened to you, Inspector, and saved both of us a deal of time and trouble. All right.

She gestures and Fremont nods and moves as though to take Charley away

Act II, Scene 1   45

At this moment the doorbell rings. They react, then the doorbell rings again

    It might be the press I suppose.
Fremont Do you want your picture in the papers? New Broom and all that?
Bligh You deal with them, Inspector.
Fremont Right.

He moves to the door, then hesitates to look back at Bligh and Charley

Bligh It so happens I *am* a black belt in karate.

Fremont exits through the house door

Bligh regards Charley

    I wish I could get into that addled mind of yours.
Charley (*touching his brow*) Perhaps it was all just one of my nightmares ... These headaches ... everything gets mixed up. But I told you the truth ... or what I thought was the truth.
Bligh And for a while I almost believed some of it.
Charley I don't expect you to believe me. Nobody does. Except George. They didn't believe me the last time. It's the best thing, to put me away ... should'na let me out in the first place. Prison's where I belong. I have sinned.
Bligh (*sighing*) Oh, Charley, Charley.

Note: at this time the scene is staged so that Charley is positioned well away from the sight line of the door, and with his back to it

    So that, as the door opens and Fremont enters with Hugo — neither Hugo nor Charley are aware of each other for a few moments

Fremont It's Mr Mead, ma'am.
Bligh (*frowning, inquiring*) Mr Mead?
Hugo Hugo. Jessica Bligh, isn't it? We've met before. As soon as I heard, I thought I must come over ... see if there was anything I could do ... I didn't expect to find the police still here — the news said you had made an arrest and ...

As soon as Hugo starts speaking, Charley reacts, turns to stare at him in amazement — until finally:

Charley (*interjecting*) George!

Hugo turns and sees Charley for the first time — he looks taken aback

> You lying bastards! They tried to trick me, George, told me you were dead, told me I was mad! Well, you can tell 'em now, can't you, George ...? You can tell 'em!?

Bligh Charley?

Charley That's him. George. Doctor Blake ... but you knew that. Why else would you bring him here ...? I'm sorry, George ... I did my best for you, but they caught me here ... I had to tell them everything. Now you tell 'em ... tell 'em about you and me, George! Make 'em believe me! You know I'm not mad, don't you, George?

Hugo frowns at Bligh

Hugo George?
Bligh Do you know this man?
Hugo No, of course not.
Charley What!? What are you saying?
Hugo Who is he?
Fremont His name's Mirren.
Charley *Charley*. We're mates, George ...
Hugo What's all this George business? Who is George anyway?
Bligh You.
Hugo Eh!?
Fremont That's what he thinks
Hugo The man must be mad.
Fremont Got it in one.
Hugo Well, I've certainly never seen him before.
Charley George.
Hugo No, wait a minute, I have seen him before — that pub in town — what is it? — *The Bricklayers*.
Charley That's right, George. (*To Bligh*) You see?
Hugo Yes, I've seen him in there a couple of times, but know him? No.
Charley Why're you doing this? Tell them!
Hugo Come to think of it, I've seen him elsewhere too ... couple of days ago, hanging around here at the end of the drive.
Fremont Did you now?

Charley stares at Hugo

Act II, Scene 1   47

Charley George? We met here, George, in this room.

Hugo looks haplessly from Charley to Bligh

Oh dear sweet Mother of God. Not another dream! (*He touches his brow*) No ... please God ... no.

Bligh and Fremont exchange a glance

Bligh Take him through to the kitchen. Fix him up with some tea or something.
Fremont Yes, ma'am. (*Gently*) Come on, Charley.

Fremont leads Charley to the house door. At the last moment, Charley turns to regard Hugo

Charley We were friends. *Mates.*

Then Fremont and Charley exit

Hugo gazes after him, then turns to Bligh and shrugs haplessly

Hugo What was all that about?
Bligh He's a bit ... you know...?
Hugo Poor bugger. (*Then, a sudden suspicion*) But what's he doing here — with you!? Is he the filthy, stinking son of a bitch who —— ?
Bligh (*interjecting with a nod*) Yes.
Hugo And you almost had me feeling sorry for the bastard. Lucky for him I didn't fall in a bit sooner ... he'd have felt my fist in his face ...
Bligh How long have you known Paul?
Hugo Oh, about three years, since I joined the dramatics society.
Bligh But Paul wasn't a member.
Hugo He was on the committee — in charge of drumming up business. Are you interrogating me?
Bligh Would you mind?
Hugo No. Not if you think it might help. But I can't see the point — you have your man, what could I add?
Bligh Just tying up some loose ends. After all, Charley — *Mirren* — did claim to know you.
Hugo And I've told you that's ridiculous. Who do you believe — me? — or a man you've just admitted is deranged?
Bligh I like things tidy, that's all. If you'd rather I discontinued this conversation ...?

Hugo No, no, fire away.
Bligh Thank you. Obviously you came to this house from time to time.
Hugo Frequently. Paul was a good friend and —
Bligh (*interjecting*) And you are familiar with this room?
Hugo What does this have to do with —— ?
Bligh (*interjecting*) Is it possible that Mirren saw you here?
Hugo I suppose so. I wasn't hiding — and I told you, I saw him lurking around nearby. Yes, he could have peeked through those windows and seen me here.
Bligh Have you ever been to Pride Street?
Hugo Pride Street? I'm not even sure where that is.
Bligh It's where Doctor Blake's consulting rooms are situated.
Hugo Doctor Blake? He mentioned that name ...
Bligh Does it mean anything to you?
Hugo No. Who is Blake anyway?
Bligh A psychiatrist. Have you ever had cause to consult a psychiatrist, Mr Mead?
Hugo Now look here —— !
Bligh (*overriding*) Have you?
Hugo No, I damned well haven't. *I've* got all my marbles.
Bligh What do you do for a living, Mr Mead?
Hugo I sell cars. Not back-lot stuff you understand. Brackley's showrooms — Rolls mostly — we don't touch anything below a Mercedes.
Bligh Thank you.
Hugo That's it?
Bligh Yes.
Hugo If you think any of that helps ...
Bligh I'll tell Diane you called.
Hugo Yes. Thanks. Well ... if there's nothing else. I'll give Diane a buzz later in the week — when she's more up to it.

He moves towards the house door — but Bligh intervenes

Bligh Be best if you and Mirren didn't meet again — so, if you don't mind ...?

She steers Hugo towards the french doors

And thank you again for your co-operation.
Hugo Any time.

Hugo exits through french doors

Act II, Scene 1   49

Bligh gazes after him for a moment, then moves to open the house door

Bligh (*calling off*) Inspector Fremont!

Bligh moves back to thoughtfully pick up and toy with the bagged pistol, then puts it back on the table

   Fremont and Charley enter. Charley enters, then stands still, surveying the area

Charley Where is he?
Bligh He's gone.
Charley Gone off and left me? No, George wouldn't do that.
Bligh (*sighing*) You are going to have to live with it, Charley. The man you saw was not George — not Doctor Blake ... and indeed Doctor Blake was dead and gone before this madness began in your mind ... Charley? *Charley?* Have you understood anything of what I've been saying to you?
Charley You've got to help me. Please, George.

Bligh and Fremont exchange a look

Fremont Christ! Now YOU'RE nominated!
Bligh There was a George, that's the only thing he seems sure of.
Fremont Course there was a George. Shared a cell for nigh-on three years didn't they? George Mickleread. Conman, bigamist, womanizer.

Bligh looks at him in mild surprise

   I burned a bit of midnight oil too, and checked him out.
Bligh Really? I thought the case was all sewn up?
Fremont It is. Was. Oh, Christ, I don't know ... he'll probably be calling *me* George next!
Bligh You're a good copper, Fremont.
Fremont Eh?
Bligh You just had to check, didn't you? I like that.
Fremont Well, I'm buggered if I do. I'll tell you, ma'am ... right now, I'd rather be playing golf!
Bligh Do you know where we can find this George Mickleread?
Fremont No.
Bligh But you have men checking up?
Fremont (*reluctantly*) Just one man. Can't we just go home now?

Bligh Yes.
Fremont Ah!
Bligh After one more question.
Fremont Oh!

Bligh moves to pick up transcript papers and consults them

Bligh Charley, we're back again to the transcript of your statement. Your story of how you first met Doctor Blake ...
Fremont Some time after he died!
Bligh Now, according to you, after you told him you were just out of prison, he made the following comment ... "Been a bad boy, have we? What have you been up to ... Flashing? Child molesting? ... Poking horses' eyes out?" Do you recall saying that, Charley?
Charley I suppose so.
Bligh More to the point, do you recall *him* saying that?
Charley I dunno. I dunno anything anymore.
Bligh "Poking horses' eyes out." Funny thing for a psychiatrist to say, don't you think?
Fremont Charley probably made it up.
Bligh In that case, it's a funny thing for *him* to say, isn't it?

Fremont stares at her uncertainly

You know the common criminal mind better than I. And Charley is certainly a common criminal ...
Fremont He's a bloody murderer!
Bligh Quite so. A bloody murderer. So why "poking horses' eyes out"? D'you ever hear that expression before? Why didn't he just say: "Do a bit of thieving"? "Stealing some wheels"? Breaking windows?

Fremont regards her — unsure of Bligh now

Well?
Fremont No, ma'am, I never heard such an expression before.
Bligh And probably — neither did Charley — so perhaps he didn't make it up, perhaps Blake *did* say that to him ...
Fremont But Blake's dead, ma'am. *Was* dead before Charley could have ever met him!
Bligh (*finally*) Yes.
Fremont Where are you leading?
Bligh I don't know. I've no idea ... except ... "poking horses' eyes out" ... I *have* heard that expression before.

Act II, Scene 1

Fremont You have?
Bligh In so many words ... and I'll tell you, George, I am not sure just how —— (*She stops short as she realizes what she has said*)

Fremont stares at her awaiting explanation

(*Almost flippantly*) Now he's got me doing it!
Fremont Yes, ma'am. (*Then*) I reckon we'll all be barmy if you ... We ... don't stop this case right now, accept what we had last night, and point him where he belongs ... behind bars. (*Then*) I'm not after my pound of flesh, an eye for an eye ... I know he's round the twist and not responsible ... but why flog a dead horse?
Bligh (*muttering*) A blinded horse.
Fremont Ma'am?
Bligh You're right. (*Then she suddenly smiles a wry smile*) I had a nanny when I was a child. Big and fat and jolly and always smelling ever so slightly of sweat.

Fremont thinks Bligh has gone mad!

She had a vulgar but vivid turn of phrase — and if ever I questioned her too long or too hard about anything she would say, "You want to know the ins and outs of a duck's arse." I think she was right, don't you, Inspector?
Fremont Well, ma'am ——
Bligh "A duck's arse." Yes. (*Then*) Right.

Fremont nods, grabs Charley, urges him to the house door, opens it and ...

Diane stands there, carrying a purse and wearing slacks and casual clothes. For a moment she regards Charley in shocked reaction, and then she screams and launches herself at him, taking both Fremont and Charley by surprise as she enters. She claws and bashes at Charley and sends him to his knees, where she uses fist, claw and feet against him

Diane Bastard!

Bligh moves in to pull Diane away — while Fremont helps Charley to his feet. Charley half covers his face with his hands — he has taken some punishment. Diane has dropped her purse

Bligh Diane! Get him out of here!

Fremont Better get him cleaned up first, or someone'll be shouting police brutality.
Bligh Just get him away!

Fremont drags Charley away to exit through the house door

Bligh holds the struggling Diane — her anger starting to subside into tearfulness now. Bligh moves her to the sofa, plumps her down, and then moves to pour a stiff drink, and returns to her with it. She waves a vague hand

Diane No ...
Bligh Drink it!

She won't be denied, and finally Diane takes the glass and drinks — starting to calm down now. Bligh picks up her purse and puts it beside her

Diane I'm sorry ... but when I saw him standing there ...
Bligh It's my fault, I shouldn't have brought him back. But then, you're not supposed to be here.
Diane I couldn't stay there. They mean well, I know that, but all that sad-eyed sympathy ... I couldn't take it any longer. What are you doing here anyway? With that man?
Bligh Going over things. Reconstructing. We'll be gone soon.
Diane (*almost strident*) Don't let me drive you away.

Bligh regards her

Bligh How much sleep did you get last night?
Diane Damned pills didn't work.
Bligh Because you fought them, just as you are fighting now the hard and awful fact that Paul is dead.
Diane Oh, Jessica ——
Bligh (*overriding*) It's something you have to do, and the sooner you do it the easier it'll be to bear. But you won't do it if you're a nervous wreck.
Diane No, I ——
Bligh (*overriding*) If you can't sleep, then at least rest. You're very close to cracking up completely, and that would help nothing.
Diane Yes, I suppose you're right. I may go away for a while. Not now, in two or three weeks' time.
Bligh So long as you're back for the trial. You'll be called you know.
Diane Oh, God, will I?
Bligh (*regarding her*) Perhaps not. I could pull a few strings. And if

Mirren stays by his confession ...
Diane Won't he?
Bligh Not for more than five minutes at a time. He chops and changes. The poor devil doesn't know himself just what ——
Diane (*interjecting*) Poor devil!? He killed Paul!
Bligh Yes, I know. Yet I can't reconcile ... He just doesn't seem like a violent man.
Diane But he's killed before, hasn't he? And children involved.
Bligh How do you know that!? Nothing's been released to the media.
Diane I ... er ... I overheard one of your men.
Bligh The times they're warned not to discuss it ..! Oh well. If I can spare you the trial you should get away — far away for a while ... Maybe South America, or a world cruise? I imagine you can afford to go anywhere you want now that —— (*She stops dead*)
Diane Yes.
Bligh I'm sorry, it was damned insensitive of me ...
Diane Paul was a rich man and it will all come to me. We both of us know that.
Bligh Lucky for you I came through that door with you last night.
Diane What? Oh, yes, otherwise I'd have been a suspect you mean? With the biggest cliché motive of them all.
Bligh No, you wouldn't have been a suspect.
Diane Oh?
Bligh Not with Mirren standing there, holding the gun. Cut and dried as Fremont would say.

Diane finishes her drink, gets to her feet

Diane I think I'll take that advice now.
Bligh Good girl. (*She embraces her*) And don't forget, day or night, I'm just a phone call away.
Diane I know.

Diane kisses Bligh's cheek, and then moves to the house door — leaving her purse, forgotten, on the sofa

Bligh Oh, by the way, Mead called.

Diane stops, turns to regard her

Hugo Mead. He came to offer his condolences and a broad shoulder if necessary.
Diane Is he coming again?

Bligh He said he would call you later in the week.
Diane It's just like him, to be first on the scene. Poor Hugo.
Bligh Poor?
Diane He's going to miss Paul nearly as much as I.

Diane exits through the house door

Bligh remains a moment, and then prowls over to the shelf that contains copies of printed plays. She starts to sort through them, looking for a title and is still so occupied when

The house door opens and Fremont pokes his head around it

Fremont Has she gone?
Bligh Yes.

Fremont pushes the door wider and he and Charley enter. Charley is holding a pad of wadded kitchen paper, beneath which is a raw steak — he holds it over his eye

Fremont Bloody hell, you'd have to be a black belt in karate knowing her! Looked as though he was going to have a right shiner, but I found some steak in the fridge, may stop it in time.
Charley Why'd she hit me?
Fremont She hit you under the Old Testament rules, Charley. Hit you because she was a mite piqued at you putting three bullets into her dearly beloved, thereby depriving him of the means to go on breathing!
Charley I didn't kill him.
Fremont Come on, Charley, I'm sick of that record, let's have the other side, eh?

During this, Bligh, disappointed at having found nothing on the shelf of printed plays, turns back into the area

Charley Well, I didn't. I couldn't kill anyone.
Fremont What about the missus and the kids, eh? You going to be telling me you didn't top them next?
Charley No, I didn't. I just said I did.

This captures Bligh's attention

Bligh What do you mean?

Act II, Scene 1   55

Fremont Now please, ma'am, don't encourage him! We'll be here all of *tonight* too.
Bligh I want to know about that first murder. His wife and children.
Fremont Once you wind him up, he'll play for hours.
Bligh I want to know what happened that time.
Fremont Then why not ask me? I was there.
Bligh You saw him do it?
Fremont No, but I found him. I *told* you.
Bligh I want to hear it from him, in his own words.
Fremont (*groans*) Oh, Christ Almighty!
Bligh Charley? Why do you think you didn't do it?
Charley Because I know, don't I? (*At Fremont*) I *was* there. I didn't kill them.
Fremont What is it you're after now — a free pardon? Compensation ...? You've done your time ...
Bligh Exactly, Inspector, he's done his time. So why should he lie now?
Fremont Because he can't help it.
Bligh Charley? If anyone is going to believe you, it's me.
Fremont Well, that makes you unique.
Bligh If you didn't do it, why say you did? Why spend all those years in prison?
Charley It was because of Moira.
Bligh Moira?
Fremont His wife.
Charley I let her down, you see. Promised I'd give up the thieving and I didn't. Brought shame on her I did ... on her and the kids. Got so that she was almost afraid to go to church, that shamed she was ... Just the shame, she went every day. Every day, rain or shine. Staunch she was, not like me. Oh, I was a believer, but she was staunch. It killed her in the end. It killed her.
Fremont *Charley*. You just this minute told us that you *didn't* ——
Charley (*interjecting*) I didn't pull the trigger, but it was me killed her. Was the death of her and my kids ... Little Sheamus and Maureen.

Fremont raises his eyes to heaven — unable to follow the contradictions

You said you might believe me. I've tried so many times to unburden myself of it. It can't hurt her now ... can it? I mean, they won't dig her up, will they?
Bligh Just tell the truth, Charley, the whole truth, from the beginning.
Charley Well, it was that morning. Early. I'd — I'd been out on a tickle ...

Bligh looks haplessly at Fremont

Fremont A job. He was out thieving.
Charley (*nodding*) She knew it too. Moira, she knew it. Knew I'd broke my promise to her. I suppose something snapped, she couldn't take it any more.
Bligh You mean, she attacked you?
Charley My Moira? Normally such a gentle creature. I found them in the kitchen, her arms around the kids, and their faces all ... all blown away. She'd took my shotgun you see and ... and ...

A long moment as Bligh and Fremont regard each other — even Fremont shaken by, and responding to, this confession

Bligh She killed them — and then herself?!
Charley I drove her to it. I was responsible.
Bligh But for God's sake, man, why on earth did you take the blame?!

Fremont heaves a mighty sigh that causes Bligh to turn and regard him

Fremont Because she was staunch.

Bligh stares at him, not understanding

   Catholics.
Charley The Monsignor at St Theresa's was O'Rourke then. Father O'Rourke, and a stony, stickler of a man he was — like a rock with a permanent frown. I know God would forgive my Moira — *has* forgiven her. And sweet Jesus, *and* the holy Mary. But never O'Rourke. It wasn't in him. That's why I lied.

Bligh is still at a loss

Fremont She was a *suicide*.
Bligh You mean they would not have buried her in consecrated ground?
Fremont Well, maybe not, I don't know in these enlightened times ... but clearly he thought not.
Charley She belonged in the ground at St Theresa's. She worshipped there every day ... even though she committed that terrible sin — her life and my kids ... it wasn't her sin, you see? It was mine. It was my guilt. Cause I'd promised, and failed her.
Bligh But you did ten years, Charley!
Charley So I feel I've paid for my sins — and hers.
Fremont Ten years! And I was the one who put you away. Damn you, Charley, this is the first thing you've ever said that I even half believe!

Act II, Scene 1   57

Bligh Do you swear, on the graves of your wife and children, that you were innocent of this crime ...?
Charley No, I told you, it was my guilt all along.
Bligh (*overriding*) Did you pull that trigger, did you physically kill them?!
Charley I couldn't kill anyone.

A moment as they take this in

Bligh Well, Inspector?
Fremont Ma'am, I don't feel well at all.
Bligh Charley, when you met Doctor Blake — George — on these numerous occasions, did you ever make this confession to him?
Charley I tried to many times, but never quite got around to it ... He wouldn't listen. Always talking — yes, a great talker is George.
Bligh So, he had no reason to doubt that you were anything other than a cold-blooded killer?
Fremont You've lost me, ma'am. What does this have to do with ——
Bligh (*interjecting*) "I couldn't kill anyone" — you heard him.
Fremont But that was ten years ago ...
Bligh No! (*Softly*) He backed a loser — backed the wrong horse ...
Fremont We're not back to bloody horses again?!
Bligh Yes, I think we are. They are vital to this case.
Fremont Do you know what I think? In a little while I'm going to see the flare of operating lights, and the pretty face of a nurse bending over me ... and then I'm going to wake up and find I was hit by a truck last Wednesday? If I'm lucky!
Bligh He is innocent of those first murders.
Fremont *He* says.
Bligh He says, and you believe.
Fremont Half believe.
Bligh Then isn't it possible he is also innocent of the murder of Paul Tulliver?
Fremont I'd like notice of that question, and a large scotch if you don't mind.

Fremont moves to pour himself a drink — then reacts as

The house door opens and Diane enters

Fremont's first thought is to protect Charley from further attack! But Diane is quite calm as she saunters over to pick up her purse from the sofa

Diane It's OK Inspector, I'm not on the rampage this time. I just want my pills ... (*she picks up her purse and shakes it*) — my sleeping pills. (*To Bligh*) Perhaps they'll work this time. (*To Fremont*) Enjoy your drink. In fact, I'll join you.

Fremont, caught with her drink bottle in his hand, is happy to comply

Bligh D'you think that's wise? You've already had a couple.
Diane And this will make three. But perhaps I need three — or even more — after what I've been through the past few hours. Thank you, Inspector.

She takes the glass from Fremont and then moves right up to regard Charley, who almost protectively holds the beefsteak pad to his eye. Fremont, too, makes a small, anxious move, but:

Diane It's all right. I told you — no rampaging.

Bligh, sensing a tension building, picks up the discarded handcuffs and moves to snap them on to Charley's wrists

Now that's what I like to see.

Bligh urges Charley towards the french doors — then glances back, reacts, and hurries over to pick up the bagged gun

Bligh Won't be a moment.

Bligh, carrying the bagged gun, exits through the french doors with Charley as she goes:

(*Calling off*) Constable Walters!

Diane gazes after them for a moment, then, sipping her drink, turns back into the area and towards Fremont

Diane That's it then.
Fremont I hope so.
Diane He's changed his story?!
Fremont To answer that accurately, I'd have to be able to remember what his story was in the first place! Nice scotch. Cheers.

He drinks — she regards him — he explains

Act II, Scene 1

It's all a bit confused.

She regards him

D'you think you could build yourself a computer? Do it yourself?

She is mildly astonished

Compared to this case it'd be a doddle!
Diane What do you mean?

Before Fremont can answer, Bligh enters through the french doors

Bligh He means that we must reconsider.
Diane Reconsider what?
Bligh Whether we have the right man or not.
Diane You're not serious? Jessica, you saw him. We came through that door together and we saw him. How can there possibly be any doubt?
Bligh Not so much doubt as unanswered questions.
Diane Such as?
Bligh Nothing to bother you with.
Diane Bother me?! Paul was my husband!
Bligh I imagine the show will go on? That's the tradition, isn't it?

Diane stares at her

The dramatic society. You'll go ahead with your usual autumn show?
Diane I don't know. I suppose so.
Bligh What are they doing this year? Not Chekhov I imagine, you did that last year.
Diane For God's sake, what does it matter?
Bligh Humour me.
Diane I — I ... something contemporary.
Bligh Farce, drama? Frayn, Stoppard, Shaffer?
Diane Yes.
Bligh Which?
Diane Shaffer. Jessica ——
Bligh (*overriding*) Not *The Royal Hunt* I hope? I found that depressing... but his comedies now ... *The Public Eye* ——
Diane (*interjecting*) *Equus*.
Bligh *Equus*?
Diane Yes.

Bligh Yes, that's exactly what I thought.
Diane What you thought?!

At this moment there are two gunshots off stage from the french doors area. They are all stunned into immobility for a moment, but then Bligh moves

Bligh Stay with her!

Bligh rushes to exit through the french doors

Fremont hurries over to gaze off after her

Diane What's happening?
Fremont I don't know.

As she moves to join him, he turns and urges her back into the room

  You'd better stay back.
Diane What's happening?
Fremont Your guess is as good as mine. Those were gunshots, weren't they?
Diane Shouldn't you be doing something?
Fremont I'm looking after you, aren't I? Perhaps somebody out there thinks the Tulliver family is in season. Anyway, there's a copper out there somewhere — *and* a karate black belt ... (*He moves back to the window*) Christ, what *is* happening?!
Diane Shouldn't you call the police?

Fremont turns to give her a long look

  I mean more police.
Fremont If necessary. We'll see. Now get back out of the line of fire.
Diane What fire? From whom?
Fremont Look, if I bloody knew I'd bloody tell you, wouldn't I? Just stay back ...

Fremont moves across the area to grab Diane and push her back against a wall

  ... there. And don't move!

Then Fremont and Diane react

Act II, Scene 2

Bligh enters through the french doors. She looks very shaken — her hands are red with blood

Bligh Call an ambulance!

Fremont does not move for a moment, just stares

He's shot one of our men. Grabbed the gun and blasted away. Well, go on, man!

Fremont hurries to pick up the phone and start dialling

Fremont Charley?
Bligh Well, of course, bloody Charley! But we'll find him — we have to. The bastard fooled me, and I was wrong, Inspector, I was terribly wrong!

Curtain

Scene 2

The same. Later that night

The area is empty and dark, lit only by the moonlight filtering through a gap where the drawn curtains over the french windows do not quite meet. All is utterly silent for a few moments and then the doorbell rings. It rings again, and then a moment later we hear vague voices

The house door opens, and Diane puts lights on and enters with Hugo

Hugo The area is lousy with coppers. Two cars down the lane, another on the way in, what's going on?
Diane You don't know?! Didn't you hear it on the radio?
Hugo Hear what?
Diane He's got away. Mirren. He's on the loose. Escaped.
Hugo Did he now? Why that's a ... it's a clear admission of guilt.
Diane He shot a policeman.
Hugo Guilty as hell. That's that then.
Diane Hugo, he's out there somewhere, running like a mad dog, with a gun in his hand. He's dangerous, and no telling what he might do next.

Hugo Yes, see what you mean. You can't stay here alone. (*With an easy familiarity he moves to pour himself a drink*) Why don't you come back to my place?
Diane I don't think that would look too good right now, do you?
Hugo No, suppose not. Then let me take you into town, drop you off at a hotel.
Diane Couldn't you just stay here?
Hugo That's different from coming back with me?
Diane Of course, quite different. After all, you're a friend of the family, came by to check up on me, and found me scared out of my wits. I *am* scared, Hugo.

He regards her

I can make up a bed for you in the back room.

He reacts — she smiles

You don't have to use it.
Hugo Damned right.
Diane Darling.

They move together to kiss and embrace, then react as there is a sudden banging at the french doors, and the drapes billow as the doors start to open. Diane stifles a scream

Constable Walters enters

Walters Sorry, ma'am, I didn't mean to startle you.
Hugo Well, you certainly did a damned good job of it!
Walters Sorry. Sorry, Mrs Tulliver. I'm Constable Walters.
Hugo What the bloody hell are you doing here? ... bursting in and ——
Walters (*interjecting*) Looking for Charley Mirren. We chased him this way, yes, he's definitely in the area ... and then, when I saw the door was open ——
Diane (*interjecting*) But it wasn't. (*To Hugo*) I locked it, I'm sure I locked it ...
Walters demonstrates that the latch is undone

Walters No, ma'am, you thought you did. But this kind of latch is tricky unless you really seat it home. It would have been easy for Charley, he's a dab hand with locks.

Act II, Scene 2

He reacts to the sound of a police whistle off stage — and a vague voice shouting:

Fremont (*off stage*) This way!
Walters I'd better check around the rest of the house! Lock these after me!

Walters hurriedly turns to exit through the french doors

Hugo quickly moves to firmly close the french doors and lock them, pulls the curtains across, then turns to where Diane stands

Diane Hugo ...?!
Hugo It's all right, it's OK, couldn't be better.
Diane What do you mean?
Hugo Copper comes and warns of killer in the vicinity. I could hardly leave now, could I? Even if I wasn't a friend of the family ... (*he moves to embrace her*) ... an intimate friend.

Diane responds for a moment, then pushes him away

Diane Better do as he said — make sure everything's locked up.
Hugo I'll do it. (*He hands her his empty glass*) You pour me another.

Hugo moves to exit through the house door. Diane remains a moment, then moves to pour another drink

While she is occupied doing this, Charley enters from behind the screen to just stand and watch her, gun in hand

A few moments pass, then Diane turns, sees Charley, and screams. She remains frozen

A few moments later the house door bursts open and Hugo enters

He stops dead as he sees Charley, is utterly shocked for a long moment and then, finally, treading warily
Hugo Charley. You got my message then?
Charley (*completely thrown by this*) Message?!
Hugo Of course you got my message — why else would you be here?

Charley just stares at him

Oh, Charley, don't say you've forgotten? After all I've been telling you these past weeks ... You must *concentrate*, Charley. Now do that for me ... it's there somewhere, isn't it? Back of your mind? Today is what day?

Charley can only stare

It's Sunday the sixteenth. And what day is that? *Charley!*

He moves to put his arm around Diane

It's our wedding anniversary. Oh, stupid of me! You've never actually met, have you? Charley, this is my wife Diane — and this is Charley — my friend. My *mate*. She's heard me talking about you so often that she insisted on meeting you at last.

Charley stares — Diane looks a bit blank too, but Hugo gives her a subtle nudge

Diane Yes, Charley I — I ——
Hugo (*interjecting*) She kept on at me. *Badgered* me. So here we all are. Now what will you have?

Charley just stares

Oh, come on, surely you'll drink our health? Scotch? Gin ... I have an excellent brandy ...? Or perhaps some champagne?! Darling, why don't you go and fetch it ...? We have some in the fridge, don't we?

Diane does not move

Don't we?
Diane (*realizing*) Oh, yes ...

Diane starts towards the house door — then suddenly Charley is galvanized — moving to put himself between her and the door — he holds the gun aimed at Diane

Hugo (*quickly*) All right, leave the choice to me. A brandy I think? Yes. (*As he pours brandy*) I see you got my gun repaired — super — what do I owe you?

Charley stops and regards the gun he holds, as though seeing it for the first time. Then he looks at Hugo

Act II, Scene 2   65

Charley George.
Hugo Yes, Charley.
Charley I — I ... What happened?
Hugo Happened?
Charley The copper. I shot a copper.

Hugo reacts and looks at Diane

Hugo Charley, not another of those dreams of yours? Not another nightmare?
Charley Nightmare?
Hugo I thought we were making such good progress too. (*He proffers a full glass*) Come on, have a drink. Put the gun down and have a —
Charley (*interjecting*) No!
Hugo What's wrong?
Charley You're not George.
Hugo Who says?
Charley You did.
Hugo *Charley*. How could that be?
Charley It was here ... right here ... I think. Yes! Earlier on today, you stood there, where you are now and she —
Hugo She?
Charley There was another person — a woman — her name was ... was Bligh.
Hugo (*to Diane*) Definitely another nightmare. Now, Charley ...

He steps towards Charley, who reacts, jerks the gun higher. Hugo freezes

   Charley, it's me, George, and I promise you're just having another of your hallucinations.

Charley still keeps the gun pointed at him

   Earlier today, you say? Well, you tell him, darling, when did I get here?
Diane He arrived just a few minutes ago.
Hugo That's right. I had to go away for the weekend ... now surely you remember my telling you about that?
Charley Away?
Hugo Yes. Since Friday night, right through until now. So you couldn't possibly have seen me earlier today. Could you?

Charley is getting more confused every moment. Hugo proffers brandy glass

    Better drive this into you, old chap. Make you feel better.
Charley I imagined it all?
Hugo Afraid so.
Charley Then I didn't kill no copper?
Hugo Of course not. You couldn't harm anyone.
Charley (*eagerly*) That's what I've been saying!
Hugo Well certainly not since you got out ... and I've been putting you to rights.
Charley It was all a dream then.
Hugo Yes.
Charley But there's things I remember —
Hugo (*interjecting*) You *think* you remember. It's all in your mind, Charley.
Charley Yes. (*Then, sharply*) But what about her? And him?

They stare at him

    That Tulliver feller. *Paul*. What happened to him?
Hugo He's living it up in New York I should imagine.

Charley reacts

    He went to America oh ... weeks ago ... don't you remember us talking about him going to America ...?
Charley I thought that was you — (*Then*) I *have* got it all mixed up.
Hugo We'll get it sorted out for you. Now come on, sit down, relax, and we'll talk about it.

Charley nods and moves towards the sofa. Hugo smiles and amiably holds out his hand

    And you'd better give me the gun, Charley.

This last remark stirs something in Charley's mind. He hesitates for a moment, but then finally hands the gun to Hugo, who is perceptibly relieved

Charley, as is usual when he is under stress, touches his brow, his face, and then reacts

Act II, Scene 2

Charley I'm bruised! (*Then*) And she did it! Yes, I remember now... Word perfect I am, I remember all of it! Got it all worked out, just how you went about it.
Hugo Oh, yes.
Charley It started that day at Doctor Blake's. Poking horses' eyes out.
Hugo Eh?
Diane Hugo, he knows ...!
Hugo This poor addled fool?! Got it all worked out, have you, Charley? Well, go ahead, tell me what you think you know.
Charley You went there that day too, had the appointment before me. They never found his appointment book, did you know that? Because you took it! Yes, you went there to see him because of a play you're going to do. I — I can't remember what it's called, but — but it's got a doctor like Blake in it ... and a boy who pokes horses' eyes out ... *Equus*! That's it. Funny name ... I don't know what it means, but it's got a doctor in it ... and that's why you went to see him ... because you were going to be a pretend doctor and you wanted to see how a real one went about it. They call it ... they call it ... (*happily*) ... research!

During this exposition, Hugo and Diane's consternation grows at Charley's astonishing insight

But when you got there, you saw them taking him away — dead or dying he was, and in the panic they left the door open ... so you went in just the same. To snoop around
Hugo (*to Diane*) Astonishing.
Charley Then I came in. And — and you saw how — how easily influenced I was. Needed a prop I did, a crutch, and that's when you decided to become George and start setting me up. (*He turns to Diane*) That's when *you* came in. Another bit of pretend just for my benefit. You wrote a little bit of a play 'specially and then asked that Paul — your husband — to help you to ... to rehearse... help you ... run it through and you made sure I was watching, and heard it all.

Charley pauses to seek the exact right phrase. Sometimes it sounds like a recitation

Diane Hugo!
Hugo Go on, Charley!
Charley Nearly there, aren't we? You put it all into my mind, including the murder. You knew I'd do anything for you to keep us from breaking up ... and it didn't even matter whether I did it or not ... because you'd

already done it. Just before I arrived. All you had to be sure of was that I was found here with the gun in my hand, and a good witness to boot ... Bligh.
Hugo Remarkable!
Charley Then you and her could live happily ever after on the proceeds. Oh, it was clever — and I was dead right, wasn't I? Who'd think otherwise than it was me who did it? After all, I'd done it before, hadn't I? But you see, what you didn't know was —
Hugo (*interjectING*) I don't know how you did it, Charley ... with your limited resources, to put it all together like that. You've really surprised me — I would never have thought you had it in you.
Charley I got it right didn't I? Word perfect.
Hugo Absolutely on the button, Charley. I'm proud of you — and grateful too.
Charley Grateful?

Hugo lifts the gun to point at him

Hugo It will make killing you just that much easier.
Diane Hugo!
Hugo We can't let him get picked up now, can we? Suppose he babbles that little story out again? And somebody starts to believe him? We can't leave him alive. I'm sorry, Charley.

He levels the gun, but Diane grabs his arm

Diane No ...

Hugo pushes her aside

Hugo I couldn't have constructed it better myself. "Dangerous killer on the run returns to scene of the crime — threatens bereaved widow, faithful friend intervenes, grapples for gun and —— "

Startlingly, he fires a shot. Charley falls down near the sofa. Diane is utterly stunned by the sudden violence. She remains frozen for a moment — and then begins to cry out in hysteria. Hugo grabs her, slaps her face, slaps her into silence

Get a hold of yourself. They'll have heard the shot, they'll be here any moment.

He hurries over to gaze down on Charley, and then lets the gun fall near the body

Act II, Scene 2

Our stories must match. He broke in here, was going to kill you ... I intervened ... the gun went off in the struggle ...

He staggers away — faking shock

I'm just as shocked as you are.

Off stage, beyond the french doors, we hear vague voices — and perhaps the sound of running feet

Fremont (*off*) Over here!

Suddenly Hugo breaks his mock-shocked pose and gives Diane a big wink and a grin

Hugo Just keep your cool and it'll work perfectly, I promise you.

Suddenly the french doors are assaulted from outside. Hugo quickly moves to unlock them

Fremont enters, to stop dead as he takes in the scene, then quickly moves to crouch beside Charley

Hugo moves to embrace and comfort Diane

Fremont What happened?
Hugo He broke in — came from there ... he was raving — was going to shoot her. I tackled him ... the gun went off ... God how awful!

Fremont climbs to his feet, holding the gun

Fremont That's the whole truth is it?

Before Hugo can reply:

Bligh (*off stage*) Not quite.

Bligh enters from hiding

Hugo and Diane react

You should be proud of Charley. Oh, the words were mine, not his, I've been coaching him all day ... but he remembered, he got it right. Well done, Charley.

Charley sits up and starts to get to his feet

Charley Thank you, ma'am.
Bligh (*calling*) Constable Walters!

Walters enters through the french doors

Diane (*to Bligh*) I saw blood on your hands ...
Bligh From one rare beefsteak. A little bit of dramatics of my own. (*To Fremont*) Sorry, I couldn't even let you in on it ... (*She moves to confront Diane*) It was a mistake you know, to blurt out that Charley had killed before ...
Diane I told you, I overheard one of your men ——
Bligh (*interjecting*) Talking about the case ... Yes. Except you don't know my men. (*Nodding towards Fremont*) They're trained experts, it's inconceivable that any of them would be so careless — and after questioning all of them I was able to confirm that ... (*She moves right up to Hugo, taking the gun from Fremont* en route) And you! You thought to use Charley as your murder weapon, but what you didn't know was that, like the blanks in this gun — he was completely harmless. (*She handcuffs Diane to Hugo*)
Diane Jessica ...?
Bligh *Take them away*!

Walters exits with Hugo and Diane

Bligh turns to regard Charley

Bligh You're free to go now, Charley. We'll give you a lift if you want.
Charley Thanks. But I'll find my own way — got to get used to that.

Charley exits

Bligh Can I buy you a drink, Inspector?
Fremont No, ma'am. (*He grins*) I'd like the privilege of buying *you* one.

And as Bligh and Fremont move to exit ——

CURTAIN

FURNITURE AND PROPERTY LIST

ACT I
Scene 1

On stage: Hi-tech shelves. *On them*: hi-fi equipment, cigarette box
Shelf. *On it*: printed plays
Low sofa covered with rug
Chair able to turn on its axis
Small, good quality desk
Desk chair
Small, iron-work table. *On it*: telephone, tray of drinks
    and glasses, pistol in clear plastic bag
Old plumbing, heating pipes etc.
Lattice screen covered with artificial flowers, plants and floral
    paper

Off stage: Small voice recorder (**Bligh**)
Desk diary (**Hugo**)
Official envelope containing papers (**Charley**)
  Writing paper (**Diane**)

Personal: **Charley**: Handcuffs
Fremont: watch, key for handcuffs
Hugo: thick-rimmed spectacles

Scene 2

On stage: As before

Check: French doors closed

Off stage: Torch (**Charley**)

Scene 3

On stage: As before

SCENE 4

On stage: As before

Off stage: Sheet of paper

ACT II
SCENE 1

Set: Typewritten papers

Check: French doors open

Off stage: Old bucket full of sand and a small trowel (Bligh)
Purse (**Diane**)
Rare steak in pad of wadded kitchen paper (**Charley**)

Personal: **Bligh**: watch, white cotton glove

SCENE 2

On stage: As before

LIGHTING PLOT

Practical fittings required: nil

ACT I, SCENE 1

To open: General interior lighting, evening. Light through french doors

Cue 1	**Bligh** switches off main lights *Fade lights to desk and immediate area*	(Page 8)
Cue 2	**Bligh** turns the lighs back on *Revert to general interior lighting, evening*	(Page 14)
Cue 2	**Charley**: "A fine sunny day." *Bring up Lights to represent a fine sunny day*	(Page 15)
Cue 3	**Hugo** and **Charley** regard each other *Slow fade to black-out*	(Page 25)

ACT I, SCENE 2

To open: Stage virtually in black-out, moonlight filtering through french doors

| *Cue* 4 | **Diane** enters and snaps on main lights
Snap on lights | (Page 26) |

ACT I, SCENE 3

To open: Stage virtually in black-out, moonlight filtering through french doors

| *Cue* 5 | The chair turns to reveal **Bligh** seated in it
Snap on lights | (Page 27) |

ACT I, SCENE 4

To open: General interior lighting, night

No cues

ACT II, SCENE 1

To open: General interior lighting, afternoon

No cues

ACT II, SCENE 2

To open: Darkness except for moonlight through gap in curtains

Cue 6   **Diane** puts lights on   (Page 61)
               Bring up Lights

EFFECTS PLOT

ACT I

Cue 1	Lighting changes to a fine sunny day *Birdsong*	(Page 15)
Cue 2	**Charley** sets the chair turning on its axis *Off stage clock chimes 10*	(Page 26)
Cue 3	**Bligh** stands up fom the chair *Off stage clock chimes 12*	(Page 27)
Cue 4	**Diane**: "... talk about him anymore just now." *Telephone rings*	(Page 35)

ACT II

Cue 5	**Bligh** pulls a white cotton glove on *Sound of car approaching*	(Page 37)
Cue 6	**Bligh** holds the gun and waits *Doorbell rings*	(Page 37)
Cue 7	**Fremont** moves as though to take **Charley** away *Doorbell rings*	(Page 45)
Cue 8	**Bligh**, **Fremont** and **Charley** react *Doorbell rings*	(Page 45)
Cue 9	**Diane**: "What you thought?!" *Two gunshots off stage*	(Page 60)
Cue 10	To open ACT II, Scene 2 *Doorbell rings, then rings again*	(Page 61)
Cue 11	**Walters**: "... dab hand with locks" *Police whistle off stage*	(Page 63)

www.ingramcontent.com/pod-product-compliance
Ingram Content Group UK Ltd.
Pitfield, Milton Keynes, MK11 3LW, UK
UKHW021845210426
5322IPUK00022B/474